Practical Mysticism

AND

Abba

VINTAGE SPIRITUAL CLASSICS

General Editors

John F. Thornton

Susan B. Varenne

ALSO AVAILABLE

The Bhagavad Gita

The Book of Job

Buddhist Wisdom: The Diamond Sutra and The Heart Sutra

The Confessions of Saint Augustine

The Desert Fathers

Devotions Upon Emergent Occasions

The Essential Gandhi

Faith and Freedom: An Invitation to the Writings of Martin Luther

The Imitation of Christ

Introduction to the Devout Life

John Henry Newman: Selected Sermons, Prayers, and Devotions

The Little Flowers of St. Francis of Assisi

The Rule of St. Benedict

Saint Thomas More: Selected Writings

A Serious Call to a Devout and Holy Life

The Spiritual Exercises of St. Ignatius

Wells of Living Water: The Five Scrolls

The Wisdom of John Paul II

EVELYN UNDERHILL

Practical Mysticism

A Little Book for Normal People

AND

Abba

Meditations Based on the Lord's Prayer

EDITED BY

John F. Thornton and *Susan B. Varenne*

PREFACE BY

Carol Zaleski

VINTAGE SPIRITUAL CLASSICS

VINTAGE BOOKS

A DIVISION OF RANDOM HOUSE, INC.

NEW YORK

A VINTAGE SPIRITUAL CLASSICS ORIGINAL, AUGUST 2003
FIRST EDITION

The text of *Practical Mysticism* was reset from a 1915 edition
published by E. P. Dutton & Company, New York; the original edition was
published in London in 1914 by J. M. Dent & Sons. *Abba* was reset from the
original 1940 edition published by Longmans, Green & Co., London.

We express our gratitude to Mr. Richard Wilkinson, on
behalf of the Estate of Evelyn Underhill, for his cooperation
and encouragement in the publication of this edition.

Library of Congress Cataloging-in-Publication Data
Underhill, Evelyn, 1875–1941.
Practical mysticism : a little book for normal people ; Abba : meditations
based on the Lord's prayer / by Evelyn Underhill ; edited by John F. Thornton
and Susan B. Varenne ; preface by Carol Zaleski.
p.   cm.—(Vintage spiritual classics)
First work originally published: New York : Dutton, 1915. 2nd work
originally published: London : Longmans, Green, 1940.
ISBN 0-375-72570-9 (trade paper)
1. Mysticism—Christianity.   2. Lord's prayer—Meditations.
I. Thornton, John F., 1942–   II. Varenne, Susan B.   III. Underhill,
Evelyn, 1875–1941. Abba.   IV. Title.   V. Series.
BV5082.3.U535 2003
248.2'2—dc21   2003047941

Book design by Fritz Metsch

www.vintagebooks.com

Printed in the United States of America
10 9 8 7 6 5 4 3 2

If the doors of perception were cleansed,
everything would appear to man as it is, infinite.
For man has closed himself up, till he sees all
things through the narrow chinks of his cavern.
—WILLIAM BLAKE

CONTENTS

ABOUT THE VINTAGE SPIRITUAL CLASSICS
by John F. Thornton and Susan B. Varenne, General Editors   ix
PREFACE TO THE VINTAGE SPIRITUAL CLASSICS
EDITION *by Carol Zaleski*   xiii
CHRONOLOGY OF THE LIFE OF
EVELYN UNDERHILL   xxxiii

PRACTICAL MYSTICISM

	Preface	3
I.	What Is Mysticism?	9
II.	The World of Reality	18
III.	The Preparation of the Mystic	29
IV.	Meditation and Recollection	42
V.	Self-Adjustment	49
VI.	Love and Will	63
VII.	The First Form of Contemplation	73
VIII.	The Second Form of Contemplation	87
IX.	The Third Form of Contemplation	102
X.	The Mystical Life	118

ABBA

I.	Introductory	137
II.	The Father	147
III.	The Name	156

IV.   The Kingdom   167
V.   The Will   179
VI.   Food   191
VII.   Forgiveness   201
VIII. Prevenience   214
IX.   Glory   227

SUGGESTIONS FOR FURTHER READING   233

ABOUT THE VINTAGE
SPIRITUAL CLASSICS

by John F. Thornton and Susan B. Varenne,
General Editors

A turn or shift of sorts is becoming evident in the reflections of men and women today on their life experiences. Not quite as adamantly secular and, perhaps, a little less insistent on material satisfactions, the reading public has recently developed a certain attraction to testimonies that human life is leavened by a Presence that blesses and sanctifies. Recovery, whether from addictions or personal traumas, illness, or even painful misalignments in human affairs, is evolving from the standard therapeutic goal of enhanced self-esteem. Many now seek a deeper healing that embraces the whole person, including the soul. Contemporary books provide accounts of the invisible assistance of angels. The laying on of hands in prayer has made an appearance at the hospital bedside. Guides for the spiritually perplexed have risen to the tops of best-seller lists. The darkest shadows of skepticism and unbelief, which have eclipsed the presence of the Divine in our materialistic age, are beginning to lighten and part.

If the power and presence of God are real and

effective, what do they mean for human experience? What does He offer to men and women, and what does He ask in return? How do we recognize Him? Know Him? Respond to Him? God has a reputation for being both benevolent and wrathful. Which will He be for me, and when? Can these aspects of the Divine somehow be reconciled? Where is God when I suffer? Can I lose Him? Is God truthful, and are His promises to be trusted?

Are we really as precious to God as we are to ourselves and our loved ones? Do His providence and amazing grace guide our faltering steps toward Him, even in spite of ourselves? Will God abandon us if the sin is serious enough, or if we have episodes of resistance and forgetfulness? These are fundamental questions any person might address to God during a lifetime. They are pressing and difficult, often becoming wounds in the soul of the person who yearns for the power and courage of hope, especially in stressful times.

The Vintage Spiritual Classics present the testimony of writers across the centuries who have considered all these difficulties and who have pondered the mysterious ways, unfathomable mercies, and deep consolations afforded by God to those who call upon Him from the depths of their lives. These writers, then, are our companions, even our champions, in a common effort to discern the meaning of God in personal experience. For God is personal to us. To whom does He speak if not to us, provided we have the desire to hear Him deep within our hearts?

Each volume opens with a specially commissioned

essay by a well-known contemporary writer that offers the reader an appreciation of its intrinsic value. A chronology of the general historical context of each author and his work is provided, as are suggestions for further reading.

We offer a final word about the act of reading these spiritual classics. From the very earliest accounts of monastic practice—dating back to the fourth century—it is evident that a form of reading called *lectio divina* ("Divine" or "spiritual reading") was essential to any deliberate spiritual life. This kind of reading is quite different from that of scanning a text for useful facts and bits of information, or advancing along an exciting plot line to a climax in the action. It is, rather, a meditative approach by which the reader seeks to savor and taste the beauty of every phrase and passage. This process of contemplative reading has the effect of kindling in the reader compunction for past behavior that has been less than beautiful and true. At the same time, it increases the desire to seek a realm where all that is lovely and unspoiled may be found. There are four steps in *lectio divina:* first to read, next to meditate, then to rest in the sense of God's nearness, and, ultimately, to resolve to govern one's actions in the light of new understanding. This kind of reading is itself an act of prayer. And, indeed, it is in prayer that God manifests His Presence to us.

by Carol Zaleski

A round blue plaque on the side of a Royal Wolver-hampton School building reads EVELYN UNDERHILL 1875–1941. CHRISTIAN WRITER AND GUIDE TO THE SPIR-ITUAL LIFE. BORN NEAR THIS PLACE. In the parish bur-ial grounds of St-John-at-Hampstead, not far from the spiritual psychologist A. R. Orage and the Llewellyn Davies boys of *Peter Pan* fame, a modest headstone commemorates H. Stuart Moore, F.S.A., and his wife, Evelyn. Between the blue plaque in Wolverhampton and the unremarkable gray head-stone in London unfolded the quietly remarkable life—spanning the late Victorian and Edwardian periods, the Great War, and the first engagements of World War II—of the woman who more than any other modern author can be credited with putting "mysticism" on the map.

Evelyn Underhill was the only child of Alice Lucy Ironmonger and Arthur Underhill, eventually Sir Arthur, a distinguished barrister who belonged to Lincoln's Inn, the oldest of the ancient Inns of Court. Sir Arthur was a renowned authority on land law, and his definition of trusts continues to be memorized by law students; but his avocation was sailing yachts. To this day the Royal Cruising Club acknowledges him as their founder and first commodore, remembering Sir Arthur as the leader of a small band of sailing enthusiasts, variously eccentric in their dispositions but united by their love of all things aquatic. From the age of thirteen, Evelyn was an avid cruiser in the family yacht, the *Amoretta,* as well as an unflappable racer of small sailing dinghies. Educated at home except for three years as a boarding student at Folkestone (1888–91), she had the freedom of her family's extensive library. She enjoyed—and as a solitary child also suffered from—a great deal of unstructured time to herself. In addition to sailing and exploring the library, she loved cats, nature study, writing, sketching, crafts, gardening, archaeology, and bicycling. Though baptized and confirmed in the Church of England, she found her family's Christian identity more notional than real. "I wasn't brought up to religion," she observed. What she *was* brought up to was an expansive interest in all manner of things. She read history and botany at King's College for Women in London, and, beginning in her teens, published short stories and poems.

Evelyn Underhill's first published book, *A Bar-Lamb's Ballad Book* (1902), dedicated to one of her cats, was a treatise in verse satirizing the legal profession, foreshadowing the blend of comic and didactic that would characterize her religious writings. In the 1904 novel *The Grey World,* she depicted the spiritual journey of a slum child who dies in misery and must work out his salvation after being reincarnated in a bleakly materialist London suburb. A year later she published a collection of medieval legends, *The Miracles of Our Lady St. Mary,* still unsurpassed as the portrait of a vibrant folk culture created and nurtured by devotion to the mother of God. Thus began a prolific and successful literary career that would yield some thirty-seven books and countless magazine and journal contributions, encompassing poetry both light and solemn, fiction, folklore, medieval history, theology, spiritual advice, and translations of ancient and modern religious texts.

She is best known for *Mysticism: A Study of the Nature and Development of Man's Spiritual Consciousness* (1911), an empathetic investigation of diverse mystical testimonies, with emphasis on their commonalities across the ages; it was the first of many works defending the mystical way of life against those who would despise it as a chimerical seduction. Her briefer work, *Practical Mysticism* (1914), was an attempt to distill the discoveries of *Mysticism* and make them accessible to a wider lay audience. She defined mysticism as "the art of union with Reality." It is everyone's vocation, and compatible with every station in life; no science can take its place, and no want of science can bar one from attaining it; for it is a way of knowing, seeing, and being, governed by the loving will rather than the logic-chopping intellect. Mysticism for Evelyn Underhill was synonymous with sanity, wholeness, sanctity, and holiness; this-worldly in its love of creation, other-worldly in its battle against the forces of materialism, cynicism, herd thinking, violence, and greed. A world without mystics, she felt, would be a dead world.

How did the daughter of a worldly barrister become so entranced with the mysteries of the spirit? On the eve of her seventeenth birthday, Evelyn recorded in her journal a set of idealistic, but rather unmystical, aspirations:

> As to religion, I don't quite know, except that I believe in a God, and think it is better to love and help the poor people round me than to go on saying that I love an abstract Spirit whom I have never seen. If I can do both, all the better, but it is best to begin with the nearest. I do not think anything is gained by being orthodox, and a great deal of the beauty and sweetness of things is lost by being bigoted and dogmatic. . . .
>
> I don't believe in worrying God with prayers for things we want. If He is omnipotent He knows we want them, and if He isn't, He can't give them to us. I think it is an insult to Him to repeat the same prayers every day. It is as much as to say He is deaf, or very slow of comprehension. . . . My motto at the present time:
>
> *Be noble men of noble deeds,*
> *For love is holier than creeds*

> Goodbye sixteen years old. I hope my mind will not grow tall to look down on things, but wide to embrace all sorts of things in the coming year.[1]

Shortly after this journal entry, upon leaving boarding school, Evelyn experienced what she called a "youthful crash": "for 8 or 9 years I really believed myself to be an atheist."[2]

The cure came through her study of philosophy. The Neoplatonism of Plotinus, the optimistic vitalism of Henri Bergson, the exuberant idealism of the German philosopher Rudolf Eucken, the symbolist mysticism of Blake, Keats, and Maurice Maeterlinck, and the Christian kabbalism of the French occultist Eliphas Levi, vindicated her intuition that there must be a Reality wider than that disclosed by our narrow ego-consciousness; this brought her to what she calls "an intelligent and irresponsible sort of theism." It was the heyday of the prewar mystical revival, and, like many other seekers, Underhill distrusted conventional piety and longed for immediate personal experience of the Spirit. Through her acquaintance with the ghost-story writer Arthur Machen, she became a contributor to *The Horlicks*

---

1. Quoted in Margaret Cropper, *Life of Evelyn Underhill* (New York: Harper & Brothers, 1958), pp. 5–6.

2. *The Letters of Evelyn Underhill,* ed. Charles Williams (London: Longmans, Green & Co., 1943), p. 125.

Magazine and met its editor, A. E. Waite, the occultist and Catholic convert famous today for the tarot deck designed under his instruction. Briefly she enrolled as a neophyte in Waite's branch of the Hermetic Order of the Golden Dawn, in which mysticism predominated over magic; there she befriended the metaphysical novelist Charles Williams.

Yet, all the while she was sampling the diverse mystical movements and visiting the fashionable esoteric salons of her day, she felt herself being drawn in by the great dragnet of classical Christianity, "half of me wishing it were true and half resisting violently all the time."[3]

Yearly travels to France and Italy with her mother, seemingly exercises in high-society tourism, became for Underhill a pilgrimage to the heart of Christian culture. At home her days were spent visiting Anglican and Roman Catholic churches; and during a week's retreat at a convent of Franciscan nuns of Perpetual Adoration, she came face-to-face with the mystery that is missing from abstract philosophical theism: the mystery of God made flesh. By 1906, she was convinced that the Roman Catholic Church, as the custodian of this mystery through the ages, was to be her ultimate home. Yet she hesitated, lingering in a "border land," as she observed in a letter to the priest and novelist Robert Hugh Benson, "half-way from agnosticism to Catholicism."

In 1907, at the age of thirty-two, Evelyn Underhill

---

3. *Letters,* p. 125.

married her childhood friend and neighbor Hubert Stuart Moore, a barrister like her father, who shared her love of nature and crafts but had little interest in her mystical pursuits and a strong antipathy to the thought of her becoming Catholic. She tried to change his mind: "I do think it must be a great gain to *you*, all round, if I can make you see the real beauties of Catholicism as well as the merely superficial corruptions on which you had been led to concentrate yourself. It is better, after all, to walk along a rather muddy path to Heavenly Syon, than not to get there at all!"[4]

But in the same year, Pope Pius X issued the encyclical *Pascendi* condemning Modernism, a radically naturalistic and antidogmatic tendency in Catholic thought. Underhill sympathized with the Modernists and felt it would betray her freedom of conscience to submit to the authority of Rome. She remained a Catholic in spirit, yet without an ecclesial home, until in the 1920s she returned to the Church of England, where she would play a key role in the retreat movement and the revival of Anglican spirituality.

Evelyn Underhill's journey from nominal Christianity to atheism, from atheism to mystical theism, and from theism to a fully realized Christian life makes a story at least as interesting as her books. It was a long pilgrimage, marked by daily prayer and meditation, arduous work on her shortcomings,

4. *Letters,* p. 59.

patient attentiveness to her parents' and husband's needs, and devoted charitable service to the poor in her city; by her emergence as a sought-after spiritual guide to seekers like herself; by her fruitful collaboration with the Bengali poet Rabindranath Tagore, with whom she translated the mystical poetry of Kabir; and by her growing indebtedness to her beloved mentor, Baron Friedrich von Hügel (1852–1925), the Roman Catholic philosopher of religion to whom she would often say she owed her spiritual life. Though Baron von Hügel was a friend of the Modernist leaders, and suffered under suspicion of being a Modernist himself, it was he who taught her to cherish the sacramental, social, and institutional life of the Church, to become more Christ-centered in her mysticism, and not to place too much stock in private experiences. After ten years of informal discipleship, she placed herself formally under the Baron's spiritual direction in 1921, soon after she made the decision to become an active Anglican.

Practical Mysticism represents an early stage in Evelyn Underhill's journey, yet it foreshadows her later discoveries. In 1924 she wrote to a young student of philosophy:

> I am glad you like *Practical Mysticism*—but please consider what is said there to be incomplete and requiring to be taken in conjunction with the sections on Institutional and Social spirituality in *The Life of the Spirit and the Life of Today*—or better still with Baron von Hügel's teaching in *Essays and Addresses on the*

Philosophy of Religion. It is only when we grasp the redemptive and creative side of spiritual life and *our* obligation in respect of it, that we escape the evil of setting up an opposition between the peacefulness of communion with God and the apparently "unspiritual" aspects of practical life.[5]

Practical Mysticism aims at wholeness, integrating one's private spiritual experiences into public mundane life; that it lacks the ecclesial and explicitly Christian notes of her mature writing is due in part to a desire to reach the unchurched seeker, the "Practical Man" she addresses, chronically busy and frazzled, and often desperately anxious and estranged, who has no time for theological niceties. Addressing Practical Man familiarly in the second person, Underhill scolds him for being excessively preoccupied with getting and having, with the hubbub and struggles of mundane existence; she then extols artists and mystics for their sublime detachment. One can imagine Practical Man's rejoinder: That's easy for you to say, since you never had to worry about making a living, or caring for children, or fighting a war. What could you know of the struggle to survive, you artists and virtuosos of the inner life?

There is much to be said in her defense. The intimate and demanding second-person address, which sounds strange to our ears, is in fact a staple of the

---

5. *Letters,* pp. 152–53.

literature of spiritual advice. One thinks of Anselm's "Come now, little man," or Thomas à Kempis's chiding, "How is it that you are so glib in excusing yourself?" There is no doubt that each of these spiritual guides is writing not only to spur on his disciples but also to scold and encourage himself. Lovingly, but without pulling any punches, Evelyn Underhill doled out such advice to the many souls who applied to her for direction; gratefully and humbly she received as much from Baron von Hügel, who did not hesitate to call her on the carpet when he felt she was spending too much time worrying about herself. In our hectic world there are few such genuine spiritual friends and masters of discernment to be found, and so we are fortunate to have books that convey something of this precious relationship.

"Practical Man" is not a term of opprobrium; rather it is Everyman, in his practical life, whom Evelyn Underhill wishes to address. She does not tell Practical Man to leave off being practical, but rather to become more truly practical by embracing the way of the mystic. In all her writings, she favors the "mixed life," in which contemplative adoration and active service are inseparably combined. The ideal practical mystic for Evelyn Underhill is a servant-saint like Florence Nightingale; had she lived long enough, she would have seen her vision of practical mysticism fulfilled in Mother Teresa of Calcutta.

Writing the preface to *Practical Mysticism* on September 12, 1914, just after the first battle of the Marne, and two days before the Great War moved into the trenches, she felt she must offer some justification. The mystical revival of the early 1900s now looked like a luxury suited to times of peace and prosperity; she even considered postponing publication. But the whole point of *Practical Mysticism* was to present mysticism as a heroic vision of life, involving a discipline as real, demanding, and fruitful as military training, like William James's "moral equivalent of war."

Coming after *Mysticism,* her weightier masterpiece, *Practical Mysticism* gives an impression of slightness, but it is heftier than it seems. Drawing upon a diverse panoply of philosophers, poets, and mystics (Plotinus, Augustine, the twelfth-century Victorines, Dante, Julian of Norwich, Meister Eckhart, John Ruysbroeck, Teresa of Avila, John of the Cross, Kabir, Kant, Blake, Keats, Wordsworth, Whitman, and Coventry Patmore, among others), Underhill miraculously distills their insights and her own into an essay that speaks unpretentiously to ordinary seekers, learned or not.

She cuts to the chase: "The spiritual life is not a special career, involving abstraction from the world of things. It is a part of every man's life; and until he has realized it he is not a complete human being . . ." (*Practical Mysticism,* preface, pp. 5–6). If ordinary life seems an unpromising terrain for spiritual progress, the fault lies with us; for ordinary life is in fact a terrible and enthralling adventure, and our failure to see it as such stems from our interior confusion and numbness. Writing to her friend and disciple Margaret Robinson in 1907, she puts it vividly: "When you are *really sure* that every bush is 'aflame with God' you will no longer feel contempt for the triviality of the bush."[6]

What keeps us from being really sure that every bush is aflame with God, *Practical Mysticism* tells us, is a conspiracy between our senses and a poorly educated imagination. We are under the illusion that the world of appearances, which constitutes only a thin portion of the "blooming, buzzing confusion" that our senses present, is the complete and factual world. We do not realize the extent to which we have made this world for ourselves by selective acts of attention. Because our affections are disordered, we dwell in a "grey world," instead of the vivid world God created; though it is fallen, the real world is much larger and brighter than the one we distractedly inhabit.

Extraordinary mystical experiences may give us a fleeting impression of the real world, and for that reason ought to be valued. They may befall us as "happy accidents" or as gracious invitations from above, but they are not an end in themselves. Rather, it is mysticism as a spiritual discipline, a martial struggle with oneself, and a prayerful waiting upon the Spirit that Evelyn Underhill recommends to us in this book. Her instructions are admirably clear: Begin with methodical daily meditation "constantly recapturing the vagrant attention," and accompany this practice of mental recollection with a balanced asceticism, comprising gentle renunciation and

---

6. *Letters,* p. 57.

unselfish service, to purify and reorient the will in the direction of one's deepest loyalties. Gradually this practice, which classical Christian mysticism calls "purgation," will bear fruit in illumination and union. It begins with methodical effort, but it ends in surrender to sheer unmerited grace. One may pass through times of aridity, but this is not to be taken as a sign of failure; as she wrote to Margaret Robinson, "the mystics don't deal with *feelings* but with *love* which is a very different thing."[7]

During the years between *Practical Mysticism* and *Abba* (1940), the second work in this volume, Evelyn Underhill became a singular force in the English church, a prolific authority on the saints and mystics of the church, and a seasoned spiritual director. In the tradition of *The Cloud of Unknowing* and St. John of the Cross, of her mentor Baron von Hügel and her friend the Benedictine abbot John Chapman, she urged her disciples to be patient with themselves during times of spiritual desolation. Thus she wrote to an anxious correspondent:

He draws us first by our own needs and longing and then afterwards, when we can stand it, to a pure love which does not even secretly desire reward. The transition, when the jam-jar is removed from the nursery table and only the loaf is left—is very bitter to our babyish spirits but *must* happen if we are to

---

7. *Letters,* p. 97.

grow up. . . . Face the fact, and trust God and not your own miserable sensations. You are being made to dissociate love from feeling and center it on the *will,* the only place where it is safe! This does not mean feeling has gone for ever, or ardour, or joy. They are to come back, at God's moment not yours, in a far better, deeper form.[8]

Like von Hügel, she would often advise the spiritually troubled to relax and trust in God, and to take up nonreligious pursuits for health and balance. Chapman's motto, "Pray as you can, not as you can't," sums up the method of this humane school of spiritual direction, which Underhill called "transcendental realism," and of which she became the leading Anglican exponent.

To Margaret Robinson, who suffered frequent attacks of what used to be called "scruples," Underhill wrote:

. . . my first impulse was to send you a line begging you only to *let yourself alone.* Don't keep on pulling yourself to pieces: and please burn that dreadful book with the list of your past sins![9]

_____

8. *Letters,* p. 231.

9. *Letters,* p. 66.

Similarly, to her dear friend Lucy Menzies:

> Don't think about being good. If you accept
> the very tiresome stuff the Lord is handing
> out to you that's all He wants at the moment.
> Let not your heart be troubled if you can help
> it, is the best N.T. bit for the moment, I think:
> but the more bovine and acquiescent you are
> the better. . . . Drop religion for the time being
> and just be quiet, and wait a bit, and God will
> reveal Himself again, more richly and closely
> than ever before.[10]

In 1935, at the historic Anglican Retreat House at
Pleshey, in Essex, Underhill conducted the retreat
on which *Abba* is based. With *Abba* and the other
retreat-talks of this period, and *Worship* (1936), her
major book on the liturgy, she established a new
point of departure for the spiritual life: She now
regarded private mystical experience as less important than the objective and corporate act of worship,
adoring God for His own sake and loving all creatures in God. In *Abba,* the cloud of witnesses expands
to include not just poets, mystics, and idealist
philosophers, but the collective voice of the Christian liturgical tradition, in all its unity-in-diversity.
Having become a devoted admirer of Russian
Orthodox worship and an ecumenical scholar of

---

10. Quoted in Cropper, *Life of Evelyn Underhill,* p. 194.

Christian liturgy East and West, she was able in *Abba* to draw inspiration from the Chaldean and Armenian rites, the Liturgy of Saint James, and the Roman Breviary.

How it would have shocked the seventeen-year-old Evelyn Underhill to know that she would one day consider it an awesome privilege and duty to be immersed in ecclesial life, to submit to the stylized forms of the liturgy, and to intone the seven petitions of the Lord's Prayer day in and day out without variation. Yet this was precisely the standpoint of *Abba*. Underhill had not lost her youthful appreciation for firsthand experience, but had acquired a new realism, simplicity, and sobriety, and had overcome the prejudice of her youth against formal and petitionary prayer.

In *Abba* Underhill meditates upon the concrete Christocentric form of worship that had eluded her in her youth. She appreciates the Jewish origins of the Lord's Prayer, its centrality within the Eucharistic liturgy, and its eschatological character; she sees it as St. Thomas Aquinas did, for whom the Lord's Prayer was "the prayer of all prayers," the summary of the gospels, and "the interpreter of desire." Handed down without alteration and deceptively familiar, the Lord's Prayer yokes together the hallowing of divinity and the longing of humanity. It is a simple formula, but also an inexhaustible mystery.

One can trace a continuous line from the young mystic who enrolled in the Order of the Golden Dawn as *Soror Quaerens Lucem* ("Sister Seeking Light") to the mature Christian who found a deeper initiation through the corporate worship of the Church. By virtue of baptism, Underhill believed, every Christian is a *Soror* (or *Frater*) *Quaerens Lucem.* Christ entrusted the Lord's Prayer not to the crowds, Underhill observes in *Abba,* but to the inner circle of disciples who were consecrated to his work. When we utter the Lord's Prayer ourselves, we are admitted to that inner circle with all its mysteries and demands:

> It is the prayer of those "sent forth" to declare the Kingdom, whom the world will hate, whose unpopularity with man will be in proportion to their loyalty to God; the apostles of the Perfect in whom, if they are true to their vocation, the Spirit of the Father will speak. The disciples sent out to do Christ's work were to depend on prayer, an unbroken communion with the Eternal; and this is the sort of prayer on which they were to depend. We, therefore, when we dare to use it, offer ourselves by implication as their fellow workers for the Kingdom. . . . (*Abba,* p. 147).

Underhill rewrote *Abba* in 1939, conscious that she was once again addressing a world facing catastrophic war. Yet, unlike *Practical Mysticism, Abba* makes no effort to defend mystical spirituality against the charge of unpatriotic quietism. By the time of *Abba,* the martial language of *Practical Mysticism* had lost its savor for Underhill. She was now a committed pacifist, dreading the conflagration to come, and intent not on politics but on first principles: adoration, intercession for the needs of the world, and loving surrender to God's will. The Kingdom of which the Lord's Prayer speaks, according to Underhill, is "the serenity of God already enfolding us, and seeking to penetrate and redeem the whole of this created order . . ." (*Abba,* p. 168). It should not be reduced to a utopian political program, for it means nothing less than "the transfiguration of the natural order by the supernatural: by the Eternal Charity" (*Abba,* p. 169).

Abba is an essay on the logic of adoration. The seven petitions of the Lord's Prayer are "seven moments in a single act of communion, seven doors opening upon 'the world that is unwalled,'" and seven aspects of the adoration and loving surrender for which we were made and by which alone we can be fulfilled. Adoration comes first, Underhill tells us, as "the one thing needful" from which everything else follows.

The key to this logic of adoration can be found, according to Underhill, in the central position of the Lord's Prayer within the Eucharistic liturgy. The Lord's Prayer is a microcosm of the entire liturgy, testifying to the divine splendor ("Holy, Holy, Holy," "Hallowed be Thy Name"), cooperating with divine providence ("Thy Will be done"), expressing creaturely contrition ("Lord, I am not worthy that you should come under my roof," "Forgive us our trespasses"), and at the heart of it all, participating in the self-offering of Christ to the Father. From the oblation at the altar to the self-offering exacted from us by daily life, we find ourselves truly only when we give ourselves away. This logic of adoration entails an ethic of adoration: "adoration . . . is the essential preparation for action." Adoration "stops all feverish strain, all rebellion and despondency, all sense of our own importance, all worry about our own success; and so gives dignity, detachment, tranquillity to our action and may make it of some use to Him" (*Abba,* p. 161).

To the extent that we are enabled to be of some active use to God, we will be in for "hard work, which soon loses the aura of romantic devotion; and must be continued through drudgery and exhaustion to the end." Underhill wrote these lines toward the end of her life, when she was experiencing drudgery and exhaustion to its fullest. Yet the keynote of *Abba* is joy. The Kingdom does not stand or fall on our own poor efforts, Underhill tells us, for it is an ever-present and prevenient reality. We are not "ring-fenced individuals" but members of the body of Christ, in whom the sanctification of the universe has already begun. The ethic of adoration dictates that we respond to God's majesty and might not with servile fear or moralistic striving but with "a deep and disciplined joy." If we are feeling exhausted and dull, then our surrender to that exhaustion and dullness may be the transfiguring work to which we are called. Underhill is speaking from her own life when she declares, "Behind every closed door which seems to shut experience from us

He is standing; and within every experience which reaches us, however disconcerting, His unchanging presence is concealed" (*Abba,* p. 231).

In an age that tends to career between skepticism and credulity, we need a third way, a way of discernment, in which a healthy skepticism about inner states combines with a trusting faith that the mystic's vision is real, and that God does indeed work in the soul. Evelyn Underhill found this third way through her life of prayer, study, and service to others; and in *Practical Mysticism* and *Abba* she offers to share it with us.

1875 Born in Wolverhampton on December 6 to Arthur Underhill, a lawyer, and Alice Lucy Ironmonger, daughter of the Wolverhampton justice of the peace, Moses Ironmonger. Shortly after Evelyn's birth, the family moves to London, where Arthur develops a successful career both as a professor and a practitioner of law.

1879 Arthur Underhill founds the Cruising Club for yacht sailing and acts as its first commodore. His daughter, Evelyn, will spend her holidays sailing and also enjoying the countryside with her family.

1888 At age thirteen, Underhill is sent to boarding school at Sandgate House, where she excels in the study of scripture and sums.

1891 Underhill is confirmed as an Anglican on March 11 at Christ Church, Folkestone.

1897 Underhill attends King's College for Women in London. She studies history and botany.

1898   During this period Underhill is essentially an unbeliever.

After leaving school, she tours Europe with her parents, as she will every spring until the start of World War I. She is particularly fond of Italy— writing descriptions and making sketches of places. These will be published posthumously. Preferring the paintings of Giotto, she complains that, by comparison, he makes all other painters seem inferior.

1902   Underhill's first book is published, *A Bar-Lamb's Ballad Book,* a collection of humorous verse about the law.

From this year until 1906, she is a member of the Hermetic Society of the Golden Dawn, an organization devoted to the exploration of experiential contact with ultimate realities through the use of ritual. Eventually she comes to spurn such attempts to achieve higher awareness through magical means because they offer no satisfaction for man's deepest desire, which is love, and because she is convinced that the way to truth is through accepting, little by little, the suffering that accompanies growing into it.

1904   Five short stories by Underhill are published by *Horlicks Magazine,* all with similar themes of the transcendental quest. *Horlicks*'s editor, Arthur Edward Waite, is a devotee of mystical texts and rituals. His influence on Underhill can be assessed by the inclusion of five of his books in the bibliography of the first edition of her masterwork, *Mysticism,* which will be published in 1911.

Underhill's first novel, *The Grey World,* is published. Through the main character, Willie, she explores her sense of a world existing beyond the one available to materialistic perspective. He discovers a potential for ecstatic experience in Catholic sanctuaries (as she did on her trips to Italy) that seemed to her to be missing from the commonsense decor of Protestant churches.

1906 Impressed by Roman Catholicism, Underhill considers conversion. However, her future husband, Hubert Stuart Moore, raises strong objections. He resents the idea that a confessor might intrude on their marital privacy.

1907 Marriage to Hubert Stuart Moore, a barrister, on July 3. Evelyn and Hubert had been friends since 1890. They suit each other well, sharing a love of country life and a devotion to cats. Hubert is talented in wood- and metalwork, for which Underhill creates designs.

The papal decree of Pius X condemning Modernism, *Lamentabili,* is published. So, too, is *Pascendi,* an encyclical letter that further castigates Modernist tendencies toward agnosticism and immanence. Underhill objects to the tone of the pronouncements though she continues to be attracted to the sacramental and mystical life of the Catholic Church.

Another novel, *The Lost World,* is published, a romance complicated by strong religious attractions, with a theme based on the atoning love of one for another.

1909   Her final novel, *The Column of Dust,* is published. The heroine, Constance, is depicted as a materialist who, nonetheless, has the gift of a consciousness of transcendence. She dreads the temptation to live in a state of illusion and despairs of the vanity and futility of her human existence. Ultimately she must reconcile her insight into the illumination that accompanies the experience of beauty with the demands of human love and the self-loss it requires. Thus the theme of redemptive action emerges, in which mysticism and incarnation are connected, as they were in the author's personal life as wife and writer.

Underhill begins to research and write the book that will define her career, *Mysticism.* She enlists the help and advice of W. R. Inge (1860–1954), dean of St. Paul's and well-known Anglican religious thinker whose own influential work *Christian Mysticism* was published in 1899. Like Underhill, he is attracted to Plotinus (204–269), the founder of Neoplatonism, who described the human potential to ascend from discursive reasoning to intuitive intelligence and, even higher, to ultimate personal unity with the supreme value that is God.

1911   Comfortably established at Camden Hill Square, Kensington, in a house left to her husband by his father, she continues to work on *Mysticism.* With her husband occupied all day by the practice of law and with the household managed by servants, she has the leisure to establish a regular routine for writing. She attends Mass frequently in Roman Catholic churches, prays the Rosary, and is especially devoted to Benediction of the Blessed Sacrament.

Mysticism is published on March 2 by Methuen and Co. The research for and writing of this book had begun in 1909. Underhill was assisted by her good friend Margaret Robinson, who was especially helpful in translating selections of writings by Meister Eckhart. In her preface to this first edition, Underhill defines mysticism as "the expression of the innate tendency of the human spirit towards complete harmony with the transcendental order; whatever be the theological formula under which that order is understood." In her preface to the twelfth edition of 1930, she insists that she would emphasize more than she had originally that "though the mystical life means organic growth, its first term must be sought in ontology—in the metaphysical Object which that subject apprehends." Drawing on the insights of psychology, she describes how the human personality is transformed as new centers of consciousness are established through the quest for fulfillment in God. Desire inflames the will, igniting the soul's determination to "taste and see that the Lord is sweet."

Underhill takes an empirical, practical, psychological approach to her subject, listing four characteristics of the mystic state of consciousness: that it is practical, not theoretical; that it is an entirely Spiritual Activity; that its business and method is Love; and that mysticism entails a definite Psychological

Experience. The faculties of intellect, feeling, and will must coordinate if one is to enter a state of prayer. As she writes in a paper on this subject ("The Place of Will, Intellect and Feeling in Prayer"): "Reason comes to the foot of the mountain; it is the industrious will urged by the passionate heart which climbs the slope." It is the whole, entire human personality that is taken up and transformed in the mystic experience.

Mysticism attracts the attention of Baron Friedrich von Hügel (1852–1925), a Roman Catholic scholar interested in mystical theology. He had founded the London Society for the Study of Religion in 1905, with which many prominent scholars came to be associated. He will greatly influence Underhill's spiritual life over the years to come.

Under the pseudonym John Cordelier, Underhill publishes *The Path of Eternal Wisdom: A Mystical Commentary on the Way of the Cross.*

1912　The great success of *Mysticism* encourages Underhill to produce a devotional work under her pseudonym, John Cordelier, *The Spiral Way, Being Meditations upon the Fifteen Mysteries of the Soul's Ascent.* She also edits and introduces for publication *The Cloud of Unknowing,* a fourteenth-century masterpiece of instruction on mystical prayer.

She writes as well an article for *Franciscan Studies* on Blessed Angela of Foglino, an Italian mystic who put herself under the protection of St. Francis of Assisi after the deaths of her husband and her five children.

At about this time she comes to know Rabindranath Tagore (1861–1941), Bengali poet and mystic who will win the Nobel Prize for Literature in 1913 and be knighted by King George V in 1915. She writes a review for *The Nation* of his poetry collection *Gitanjali*. Friedrich von Hügel also now enters her life. His work, *Mystical Element in Religion* (1908), greatly influences Underhill.

1913 In March, *The Mystic Way* is published with the subtitle "A Psychological Study in Christian Origins." Underhill is greatly informed and influenced in the writing of this book by Henri-Louis Bergson (1859–1941), who will become a Nobel laureate in literature in 1927. Famous for his theory of the *élan vital,* or current of consciousness, which he saw as the impetus for evolutionary development, Bergson believed that God manifests Himself through intuitive illuminations rather than intellectualized dogmas. Using the *élan vital* as a hermeneutical principle, Underhill presents Jesus as the exemplar or archetype of mystical consciousness that succeeds in perfect self-transcendence through total submission to the Universal Will. The popularity of Underhill's books and others like them indicates a general public interest in the nature and psychology of human consciousness and its relation to the whole of life.

Underhill writes again for *The Nation,* reviewing Tagore's *Sadhana: The Realization of Life* and *The Crescent Moon, Child Poems*.

Underhill is elected a fellow of Queen's College

for Women. She is now a major figure on the contemporary religious scene.

1914   World War I breaks out. Underhill remains in London with her husband and works for Naval Intelligence translating guidebooks on Africa. The house next door to theirs is bombed, and Lincoln's Inn, where her husband works, is left in ruins. Two young nephews are killed at the front. Hubert uses his practical intelligence to help in the development of artificial limbs.

Practical Mysticism: A Little Book for Normal People is published on August 4, just as the war breaks out. In the preface, dated September 14, Underhill defends the necessity of the role of mysticism as the evil and brutality of war engulfs the world, i.e., "to see the world in a truer proportion, discerning eternal beauty beyond and beneath apparent ruthlessness." The virile mystic is an active "struggling, fighting soul whom the Early Christians called an athlete of the Spirit," a Joan of Arc.

She assists in editing an English translation of *The Autobiography of Maharshi Devendranath Tagore,* father of Rabindranath Tagore, for which she provides a lengthy introduction. She situates him within the religious framework of India and demonstrates points of similarity and resonance with the mystics of the West.

Underhill provides the introduction for a new edition of *The Fire of Love or Melody of Love,* by Richard Rolle. Rolle (c. 1300–49) was a late Middle

English mystical writer and hermit whose contemplative focus was centered on taking joy in the life of Jesus. Underhill admires Rolle for his passionate feeling and sweetness.

1915   Underhill collaborates with Tagore to publish a translation of, and writes an introduction to, the mystical lyrics of the fifteenth-century Bengali poet Kabir. (It is now known that the poems collected here are not those of Kabir himself.)

1916   Underhill's second volume of collected verse, *Theophanies,* is published by J. M. Dent & Sons, who, in 1912, had brought out her first volume, *Immanence.* Her poems express her intuition of a sacramental indwelling in nature by God. In addition to Bergson, she was influenced by Johannes Scotus Erigena (c. 810–c. 877), foremost religious thinker of the early Middle Ages, who had written: "Every visible and invisible creature is a theophany or appearance of God."

Some of her poems are included in *The Oxford Book of Mystical Verse* (1917) along with those of Arthur Waite, Francis Thompson, R. H. Benson, Alice Meynell, James Stephens, and John Masefield.

John of Ruysbroeck: The Adornment of the Spiritual Marriage, The Sparkling Stone, The Book of Supreme Truth, a three-volume work, is published and is edited and introduced by Underhill. Ruysbroeck (1293–1381) taught that in the true deification of the soul, one is not subsumed into God but, rather, maintains true personal identity. Christian perfection is attained by passing through three stages: the active life, the inward life, and the contemplative life.

1918 Underhill's articles this year include "The Future of Mysticism," published in *Everyman;* "The Mystery of Plotinus," in *The Quarterly Review;* and a review of W. R. Inge's *The Philosophy of Plotinus.*

1919 Underhill publishes *Jacopone da Todi, Poet and Mystic 1228–1306: A Spiritual Biography.* Jacopone, an Italian Franciscan tertiary (a member of a monastic order who takes only simple vows and may live outside the cloister and may own property), wrote spiritual ballads suffused with hope and joy, fear and desolation, exaltation and self-denigration, which greatly appeal to Underhill.

1920 Underhill continues her work of editing and popularizing the writings of the mystics, including the Flemish Jan Van Ruysbroeck (1293–1381), the anonymous fourteenth-century treatise *The Cloud of Unknowing,* and *The Scale of Perfection,* by Walter Hilton, the fifteenth-century Augustinian canon. She writes to a friend that Ruysbroeck is her personal favorite.

Underhill writes reviews of works by Julian of Norwich and St. Thérèse of Lisieux, and an introduction to *The Confessions of Jacob Boehme.* A collection of her previously published articles, *The Essentials of Mysticism and Other Essays,* is published.

Her morning routine is occupied by her writing;

her afternoons by letter writing, visits to the poor, and the work of spiritual direction.

1921 Underhill becomes an active member of the Church of England after being profoundly edified by the blessed death of her good friend Ethel Ross Baker, who died after much suffering still firm in her Catholic faith. Baron Friedrich von Hügel officially becomes her spiritual director. Though Roman Catholic himself, out of respect for her husband's wishes, he does not encourage her conversion from Anglicanism. He is greatly helpful to her as she battles with her tendency to be overly self-reproachful. He leads her to reconcile her thirst for the pure mysticism of exclusive concentration on God with the need to live in a social, familial, and marital milieu. He encourages her to become more centered on Christ in her prayer and devotion so as to live out a practical charity anchored in her concrete, human world.

Underhill seeks guidance from von Hügel now, as she will in the years to come, regarding visions, illuminations, and voices. The fact that she has some certainty about their validity does not, however, prevent her from being deeply doubtful and skeptical about their authenticity. The baron encourages her not to base her faith on such experiences but to hold fast to belief in God and Christ and the need to die to self in order to enter into His redemptive work.

She delivers the first of the Upton Lectures and thus is the first woman to appear on the Oxford University list of honorary speakers.

1922   The Upton Lectures are published under the title *The Life of the Spirit and the Life of Today*. She also publishes *Degrees of Prayer* in pamphlet form. They give evidence of her turn to the importance of institutional membership and liturgical prayer.

She attends her first retreat at Pleshey Retreat House, a former Anglican convent near London.

1923   Evelyn provides the introduction to a newly edited edition of *The Scale of Perfection,* by Walter Hilton (d. 1395 or 1396), Canon Regular of St. Augustine at Thurgarton. Hilton's work, a doctrine of ascetical and mystical devotion, was written to encourage holiness of life for all baptized Christians. Hilton broke with the tradition that confined prayer and perfection to those living the cloistered life. His book was first printed in 1494.

1924   At Pleshey Retreat House, Underhill conducts her first retreat, for which she is prepared by Baron von Hügel.

Her mother dies in April. Although Evelyn, an only child, had taken tea daily with her mother and they had vacationed together each year, her mother never did share her interest in spiritual matters.

1925   Baron von Hügel dies in January. He had been Underhill's refuge and guide in her spiritual sufferings, which consisted largely of surging temptations to jealousy over friendships, to bitterness, and to possessiveness. His advice had been to encourage her to practice detachment and self-forgetfulness.

He had also encouraged her to lessen her workload as he saw that it led to stress and strain on her spirit.

The Mystics of the Church is published. Defining mystical experience as "first-hand knowledge of God," Underhill shows how various Christians throughout history, including Luther, Boehme, Blake, and William Law, as well as Catholics, have lived in the presence of the Divine Spirit and Love.

1926 In tribute to von Hügel, Underhill writes a review of his *Essays and Addresses on the Philosophy of Religion* for *The Spectator.*

Walter Howard Frere, Bishop of Truro, becomes Underhill's spiritual director. A pastoral, good-hearted man, he is practical and dutiful rather than mystical in his religious sensibility.

Underhill writes a review for *The Spectator* of Paul Van Dyke's book, *Ignatius Loyola.* St. Ignatius of Loyola (1491–1556), founder of the Society of Jesus and author of *Spiritual Exercises,* attracts Underhill with his emphasis on giving glory to God, recognizing that we come from God and will return to God. The aim of the *Exercises* influences her own retreats, i.e., "To conquer self and order life without exaggerated affection."

Underhill's addresses to the Liverpool clergy are published as *Concerning the Inner Life.*

1927 A collection of papers and addresses given between 1922 and 1927 is published under the title *Man and the Supernatural.* They share a common theme of Underhill's reaction against the tendency to a "social Christianity," along with her call for a return to individual devotional prayer as the fount from which genuine saving action should spring.

Underhill is made a fellow of King's College, London. She addresses the Anglo-Catholic Congress, its only female speaker.

1928   Underhill writes the introduction for a translation of Nicholas of Cusa's *The Vision of God*. Nicholas Krebs of Cusa (1401–64) was a German theologian and diplomat for the Catholic Church. A Neoplatonist, he rejected the Aristotelian logic and dialectic that pervaded Europe in the thirteenth century. Instead, he taught a mystical theology based on his theory that reality is permeated by the infinite and that all instances of being are reflections of divine reality.

1929   Underhill's *The House of the Soul* is published. She becomes religion editor of *The Spectator*.

1930   Underhill begins to experience chronic ill health stemming from an asthmatic condition, though her active life of writing, giving retreats, and socializing continues unabated. She devotes much time and energy to preparing the twelfth edition of *Mysticism*. It reflects her religious development under von Hügel. Her explicit personal devotion to God alone is now balanced by the self-abnegation required to live one's daily life in a spirit of love and compassion for others. Newly quoted thinkers include Rudolf Otto, Henri Bremond, Jacques Maritain, and A. Poulain. Heavily edited or eliminated are passages from Rudolf Steiner, Arthur Machen, Henri Bergson, and Arthur Waite. She includes more material from the New Testament and St. Paul.

1931 Underhill continues to write articles and reviews as well as to broadcast addresses on the radio. She is sought after as a spiritual director and gives as many as eight retreats a year. She writes an introduction for Lucy Menzies's translation of *A Simple Method of Raising the Soul to Contemplation in the Form of a Dialogue,* by Francois Malaval (1627–1719), a blind French contemplative known for his holiness of life. Menzies, her good friend and collaborator, will edit several posthumous works of Underhill.

1932 Underhill's theory of unitive prayer is fully expressed in *The Golden Sequence: A Four-Fold Study of the Spiritual Life,* in which she insists that adoration of God should be the first focus of public worship as well as of private prayer. Adoration is the very soul of prayer, which produces cooperation of the Christian in God's intentions for the world. Here we find Underhill's synthesis of contemplation and action.

The Reverend Reginald Somerset Ward, an Anglican priest, now becomes her spiritual director. She appreciates his psychological as well as spiritual intuition, finding that his methods of direction are very much like those of Baron von Hügel. She describes him as "a specialist working for the Love of

God & brimming over with common sense!" He will outlive her, dying in 1962 at the age of eighty-one.

1933   A collection of Underhill's conferences is published under the title *Mixed Pasture: Twelve Essays and Addresses.*

1934   Underhill brings out *The School of Charity: Meditations on the Christian Creed.* During this period she is working intensively on *Worship.* After *Mysticism,* it will become her most important book.

1935   Underhill publishes two reviews of *The Spiritual Letters of Dom John Chapman,* one in *The Criterion* and the other in *Theology.* Chapman (1865–1933) was baptized Henry Palmer. First an Anglican deacon and then a Catholic, he is a Benedictine biblical scholar. His hypothesis of a mystical faculty, damaged but not eliminated by the Fall and common to all men, is of great interest to Underhill.

1936   Underhill's great work, *Worship,* is published as part of a series, the Library of Constructive Theology, under the general editors W. R. Matthews and H. Wheeler Robinson. For three years she had concentrated nearly all her energy on its production. After years of agonizing over the problems of self-suggestion in prayer, she had come to a full appreciation of man's dependence on sacrament and ritual to approach the transcendent. It is the liturgical work of the Church to help one overcome the ego-centric inclinations of human nature. The book is well received by both Anglicans and Catholics as well as by the Orthodox community.

Underhill gives her last retreat, which will be published posthumously in 1942 under the title *The Fruits of the Spirit*. A radio broadcast from earlier in the year is published as a pamphlet called *What Is Mysticism?*

1937 Four more radio talks are published under the title *The Spiritual Life*. Underhill's health is weakening fast, and she is often confined to bed for extended periods of time.

1938 Underhill is awarded an honorary doctorate in theology from the University of Aberdeen. She is too ill to receive it in person.

The Mystery of Sacrifice: A Meditation on the Liturgy is published.

1939 As war in Europe approaches, Underhill expresses her strong support of the cause of pacifism in several publications, believing that Christian love must find an alternative to war.

Underhill's father, Hubert, dies in June.

1940 Underhill's *Abba: Meditations Based on the Lord's Prayer* is published.

1941 The last of Underhill's many essays, a review of Charles Williams's *Witchcraft,* is published in *Time and Tide.*

Underhill develops a hematoma in her neck in the late spring. After four weeks of suffering she dies at Lawn House in Hampstead on June 15. She is buried from Christ Church, Folkestone, and rests in the graveyard of St. John's Parish Church in Hampstead.

Practical

Mysticism

TO THE UNSEEN FUTURE

PREFACE

This little book, written during the last months of peace, goes to press in the first weeks of the Great War. Many will feel that in such a time of conflict and horror, when only the most ignorant, disloyal, or apathetic can hope for quietness of mind, a book which deals with that which is called the "contemplative" attitude to existence is wholly out of place. So obvious, indeed, is this point of view, that I had at first thought of postponing its publication. On the one hand, it seems as though the dreams of a spiritual renaissance, which promised so fairly but a little time ago, had perished in the sudden explosion of brute force. On the other hand, the thoughts of the English race are now turned, and rightly, toward the most concrete forms of action—struggle and endurance, practical sacrifices, difficult and long-continued effort—rather than toward the passive attitude of self-surrender which is all that the practice of mysticism seems, at first sight, to demand. Moreover, that deep conviction of the dependence of all human worth upon eternal values, the immanence of the Divine Spirit within the human soul, which lies at the root of a mystical concept of life, is hard indeed to reconcile with much of the human history now being poured red-hot from the cauldron of war. For all these reasons, we are likely during the present crisis to witness a revolt from those superficially mystical notions which threatened to become too popular during the immediate past.

Yet, the title deliberately chosen for this book—that of *Practical Mysticism*—means nothing if the attitude and the discipline which it recommends be adapted to fair weather alone, if the principles for which it stands break down when subjected to the pressure of events, and cannot be reconciled with the sterner duties of the national life. To accept this position is to reduce mysticism to the status of a spiritual plaything. On the contrary, if the experiences on which it is based have indeed the transcendent value for humanity which the mystics claim for them—if they reveal to us a world of higher truth and greater reality than the world of concrete happenings in which we seem to be immersed—then that value is increased rather than lessened when confronted by the overwhelming disharmonies and sufferings of the present time. It is significant that many of these experiences are reported to us from periods of war and distress: that the stronger the forces of destruction appeared, the more intense grew the spiritual vision which opposed them. We learn from these records that the mystical consciousness has the power of lifting those who possess it to a plane of reality which no struggle, no cruelty, can disturb: of conferring a certitude which no catastrophe can wreck. Yet it does not wrap its initiates in a selfish and other-worldly calm, isolate them from the pain and effort of the common life. Rather, it gives them renewed vitality, administering to the human spirit not—as some suppose—a soothing draft, but the most powerful of stimulants. Stayed upon eternal realities, that spirit will be far better able to endure and profit by the stern discipline which the race is now called to undergo, than those who are wholly at the mercy of events; better able to discern the real from the illusory issues, and to pronounce judgment on the new problems, new difficulties, new fields of activity now disclosed. Perhaps it is worthwhile to remind ourselves that the two women who have left the deepest mark upon the military history of France and England—Joan of Arc and Florence Nightingale—both acted under mystical compulsion. So, too, did one of the noblest of modern soldiers, General Gordon. Their national value was directly connected with their deep spiritual consciousness: their intensely practical energies were the flowers of a contemplative life.

We are often told that in the critical periods of history it is the national soul which counts: that "where there is no vision, the people perish." No nation is truly defeated which retains its spiritual self-possession. No nation is truly victorious which does not emerge with soul unstained. If this be so, it becomes a part of true patriotism to keep the spiritual life, both of the individual citizen and of the social group, active and vigorous, its vision of realities unsullied by the entangled interests and passions of the time. This is a task in which all may do their part. The spiritual life is not a special career, involving abstraction from the world of things. It is a part of every man's life; and until he has realized it he is not a complete human being, has not entered into possession of all his powers. It is therefore the function of a practical mysticism to increase, not diminish, the total efficiency, the wisdom and steadfastness, of those who try to practice it. It will help them to enter, more completely than ever before, into the life of the group to which they belong. It will teach them to see the world in a truer proportion, discerning eternal beauty beyond and beneath apparent ruthlessness. It will educate them in a charity free from all taint of sentimentalism; it will confer on them an unconquerable hope and assure them that still, even in the hour of greatest desolation, "There lives the dearest freshness deep down things."[1]

As a contribution, then, to these purposes, this little book is now published. It is addressed neither to the learned nor to the devout, who are already in possession of a wide literature dealing from many points of view with the experiences and philosophy of the mystics. Such readers are warned that they will find here nothing but the restatement of elementary and familiar propositions, and invitations to a discipline immemorially old. Far from presuming to instruct those to whom firsthand information is both accessible and palatable, I write only for the

---

1. From the sonnet "God's Grandeur," by Gerald Manley Hopkins. (Eds.)

larger class which, repelled by the formidable appearance of more elaborate works on the subject, would
yet like to know what is meant by mysticism, and
what it has to offer to the average man: how it helps
to solve his problems, how it harmonizes with the
duties and ideals of his active life. For this reason, I
presuppose in my readers no knowledge whatever
of the subject, either upon the philosophic, religious,
or historical side. Nor, since I wish my appeal to be
general, do I urge the special claim of any one theological system, any one metaphysical school. I have
merely attempted to put the view of the universe
and man's place in it which is common to all mystics
in plain and untechnical language, and to suggest
the practical conditions under which ordinary persons may participate in their experience. Therefore
the abnormal states of consciousness which sometimes appear in connection with mystical genius are
not discussed: my business being confined to the
description of a faculty which all men possess in a
greater or less degree.

The reality and importance of this faculty are
considered in the first three chapters. In the fourth
and fifth is described the preliminary training of
attention necessary for its use; in the sixth, the general self-discipline and attitude toward life which it
involves. The seventh, eighth, and ninth chapters
treat in an elementary way of the three great forms
of contemplation; and in the tenth, the practical
value of the life in which they have been actualized
is examined. Those kind enough to attempt the

perusal of the book are begged to read the first sections with some attention before passing to the latter part.

E. U.

September 12, 1914

Chapter I
WHAT IS MYSTICISM?

Those who are interested in that special attitude toward the universe which is now loosely called "mystical" find themselves beset by a multitude of persons who are constantly asking—some with real fervor, some with curiosity, and some with disdain— "What *is* mysticism?" When referred to the writings of the mystics themselves, and to other works in which this question appears to be answered, these people reply that such books are wholly incomprehensible to them.

On the other hand, the genuine inquirer will find before long a number of self-appointed apostles who are eager to answer his question in many strange and inconsistent ways, calculated to increase rather than resolve the obscurity of his mind. He will learn that mysticism is a philosophy, an illusion, a kind of religion, a disease; that it means having visions, performing conjuring tricks, leading an idle, dreamy, and selfish life, neglecting one's business, wallowing in vague spiritual emotions, and being "in tune with the infinite." He will discover that it emancipates him from all dogmas—sometimes from all morality—and at the same time that it is very superstitious. One expert tells him that it is simply "Catholic piety," another that Walt Whitman was a typical mystic; a third assures him that all mysticism comes from the East, and supports his statement by an appeal to the mango trick.[2] At the end of a prolonged course of lectures, sermons, tea parties, and talks with earnest persons, the inquirer is still heard saying—too often in tones of exasperation—"What *is* mysticism?"

Not easy to define

I dare not pretend to solve a problem which has provided so much good hunting in the past. It is indeed the object of this little essay to persuade the practical man to the one satisfactory course: that of discovering the answer for himself. Yet perhaps it will give confidence if I confess at the outset that I have discovered a definition which to me appears to cover all the ground, or at least, all that part of the ground which is worth covering. It will hardly stretch to the mango trick; but it finds room at once for the visionaries and the philosophers, for Walt Whitman and the saints.

Here is the definition:

Mysticism is the art of union with Reality. The mystic is a person who has attained that union in greater or less degree, or who aims at and believes in such attainment.

It is not expected that the inquirer will find great comfort in this sentence when first it meets his eye. The ultimate question, "What is Reality?"—a ques-

---

2. Probably an allusion to an Indian street magician's trick whereby a mango seed is mysteriously conjured into a living tree. (Eds.)

tion, perhaps, which never occurred to him before—
is already forming in his mind; and he knows that it
will cause him infinite distress. Only a mystic can
answer it, and he, in terms which other mystics alone
will understand. Therefore, for the time being, the
practical man may put it on one side. All that he is
asked to consider now is this: that the word *union*
represents not so much a rare and unimaginable
operation, as something which he is doing, in a
vague, imperfect fashion, at every moment of his
conscious life; and doing with intensity and thor-
oughness in all the more valid moments of that life.
We know a thing only by uniting with it; by assimilating it; by an interpenetration of it and ourselves.
It gives itself to us, just insofar as we give ourselves
to it; and it is because our outflow toward things is
usually so perfunctory and so languid that our comprehension of things is so perfunctory and languid
too. The great Sufi who said that "Pilgrimage to the
place of the wise is to escape the flame of separation" spoke the literal truth. Wisdom is the fruit of
communion; ignorance the inevitable portion of
those who "keep themselves to themselves," and
stand apart, judging, analyzing the things which
they have never truly known.

Because he has surrendered himself to it, "united"
with it, the patriot knows his country, the artist
knows the subject of his art, the lover his beloved,
the saint his God, in a manner which is inconceivable as well as unattainable by the looker-on. Real
knowledge, since it always implies an intuitive sympathy more or less intense, is far more accurately

suggested by the symbols of touch and taste than by those of hearing and sight. True, analytic thought follows swiftly upon the contact, the apprehension, the union: and we, in our muddle-headed way, have persuaded ourselves that this is the essential part of knowledge—that it is, in fact, more important to cook the hare than to catch it. But when we get rid of this illusion and go back to the more primitive activities through which our mental kitchen gets its supplies, we see that the distinction between mystic and nonmystic is not merely that between the rationalist and the dreamer, between intellect and intuition. The question which divides them is really this: What, out of the mass of material offered to it, shall consciousness seize upon—with what aspects of the universe shall it "unite"?

It is notorious that the operations of the average human consciousness unite the self, not with things as they really are, but with images, notions, aspects of things. The verb "to be," which he uses so lightly, does not truly apply to any of the objects among which the practical man supposes himself to dwell. For him the hare of Reality is always ready-jugged:[3] he conceives not the living, lovely, wild, swift-moving creature which has been sacrificed in order that he may be fed on the deplorable dish which he calls "things as they really are." So complete, indeed, is the separation of his consciousness from the facts of being, that he feels no sense of loss. He is happy

---

3. I.e., cooked in a casserole. (Eds.)

enough "understanding," garnishing, assimilating the carcass from which the principle of life and growth has been ejected, and whereof only the most digestible portions have been retained. He is not "mystical."

But sometimes it is suggested to him that his knowledge is not quite so thorough as he supposed. Philosophers in particular have a way of pointing out its clumsy and superficial character; of demonstrating the fact that he habitually mistakes his own private sensations for qualities inherent in the mysterious objects of the external world. From those few qualities of color, size, texture, and the rest, which his mind has been able to register and classify, he makes a label which registers the sum of his own experiences. This he knows, with this he "unites"; for it is his own creature. It is neat, flat, unchanging, with edges well defined: a thing one can trust. He forgets the existence of other conscious creatures, provided with their own standards of reality. Yet the sea as the fish feels it, the borage as the bee sees it, the intricate sounds of the hedgerow as heard by the rabbit, the impact of light on the eager face of the primrose, the landscape as known in its vastness to the wood louse and ant—all these experiences, denied to him forever, have just as much claim to the attribute of Being as his own partial and subjective interpretations of things.

Because mystery is horrible to us, we have agreed for the most part to live in a world of labels; to make of them the current coin of experience, and ignore their merely symbolic character, the infinite gradation of values which they misrepresent. We simply do not attempt to unite with Reality. But now and then that symbolic character is suddenly brought home to us. Some great emotion, some devastating visitation of beauty, love, or pain, lifts us to another level of consciousness; and we are aware for a moment of the difference between the neat collection of discrete objects and experiences which we call the world, and the height, the depth, the breadth of that living, growing, changing Fact, of which thought, life, and energy are parts, and in which we "live and move and have our being." Then we realize that our whole life is enmeshed in great and living forces, terrible because unknown. Even the power which lurks in every coal scuttle, shines in the electric lamp, pants in the motor-omnibus, declares itself in the ineffable wonders of reproduction and growth, is supersensual. We do but perceive its results. The more sacred plane of life and energy which seems to be manifested in the forces we call "spiritual" and "emotional"—in love, anguish, ecstasy, adoration—is hidden from us too. Symptoms, appearances, are all that our intellects can discern: sudden irresistible inroads from it, all that our hearts can apprehend. The material for an intenser life, a wider, sharper consciousness, a more profound understanding of our own existence, lies at our gates. But we are separated from it, we cannot assimilate it; except in abnormal moments, we hardly know that it is there.

We now begin to attach at least a fragmentary meaning to the statement that "mysticism is the art

of union with Reality." We see that the claim of such
a poet as Whitman to be a mystic lies in the fact
that he has achieved a passionate communion with
deeper levels of life than those with which we usually deal—has thrust past the current notion to the
Fact: that the claim of such a saint as Teresa[4] is
bound up with her declaration that she has achieved
union with the Divine Essence itself. The visionary
is a mystic when his vision mediates to him an actuality beyond the reach of the senses. The philosopher is a mystic when he passes beyond thought to
the pure apprehension of truth. The active man is a
mystic when he knows his actions to be a part of a
greater activity. Blake, Plotinus, Joan of Arc, and
John of the Cross—there is a link which binds all
these together: but if he is to make use of it, the
inquirer must find that link for himself. All four
exhibit different forms of the working of the contemplative consciousness, a faculty which is proper
to all men, though few take the trouble to develop
it. Their attention to life has changed its character,
sharpened its focus: and as a result they see, some
a wider landscape, some a more brilliant, more significant, more detailed world than that which is
apparent to the less educated, less observant vision
of common sense.

The old story of Eyes and No-Eyes is really the
story of the mystical and unmystical types. "No-

---

4. St. Teresa of Avila (1515–82), Spanish Carmelite nun and
mystic. (Eds.)

Eyes" has fixed his attention on the fact that he is obliged to take a walk. For him the chief factor of existence is his own movement along the road; a movement which he intends to accomplish as efficiently and comfortably as he can. He asks not to know what may be on either side of the hedges. He ignores the caress of the wind until it threatens to remove his hat. He trudges along, steadily, diligently, avoiding the muddy pools, but oblivious of the light which they reflect. "Eyes" takes the walk too: and for him it is a perpetual revelation of beauty and wonder. The sunlight inebriates him, the winds delight him, the very effort of the journey is a joy. Magic presences throng the roadside, or cry salutations to him from the hidden fields. The rich world through which he moves lies in the foreground of his consciousness; and it gives up new secrets to him at every step. "No-Eyes," when told of his adventures, usually refuses to believe that both have gone by the same road. He fancies that his companion has been floating about in the air, or beset by agreeable hallucinations. We shall never persuade him to the contrary unless we persuade him to look for himself.

Therefore it is to a practical mysticism that the practical man is here invited: to a training of his latent faculties, a bracing and brightening of his languid consciousness, an emancipation from the fetters of appearance, a turning of his attention to new levels of the world. Thus he may become aware of the universe which the spiritual artist is always trying to disclose to the race. This amount of mystical perception—this "ordinary contemplation," as the specialists call it—is possible to all men: without it, they are not wholly conscious, nor wholly alive. It is a natural human activity, no more involving the great powers and sublime experiences of the mystical saints and philosophers than the ordinary enjoyment of music involves the special creative powers of the great musician.

As the beautiful does not exist for the artist and poet alone—though these can find in it more poignant depths of meaning than other men—so the world of Reality exists for all; and all may participate in it, unite with it, according to their measure and to the strength and purity of their desire. "For heaven ghostly," says *The Cloud of Unknowing,*[5] "is as nigh down as up, and up as down; behind as before, before as behind, on one side as other. Inasmuch, that whoso had a true desire for to be at heaven, then that same time he were in heaven ghostly. For the high and the next way thither is run by desires, and not by paces of feet." None therefore is condemned, save by his own pride, sloth, or perversity, to the horrors of that which Blake called "single vision"— perpetual and undivided attention to the continuous cinematograph performance which the mind has conspired with the senses to interpose between ourselves and the living world.

5. An anonymous work of medieval mysticism. (Eds.)

The practical man may justly observe at this point that the world of single vision is the only world he knows; that it appears to him to be real, solid, and self-consistent; and that until the existence—at least, the probability—of other planes of reality is made clear to him, all talk of uniting with them is mere moonshine, which confirms his opinion of mysticism as a game fit only for idle women and inferior poets. Plainly, then, it is the first business of the missionary to create, if he can, some feeling of dissatisfaction with the world within which the practical man has always lived and acted; to suggest something of its fragmentary and subjective character. We turn back therefore to a further examination of the truism—so obvious to those who are philosophers, so exasperating to those who are not—that man dwells, under normal conditions, in a world of imagination rather than a world of facts; that the universe in which he lives and at which he looks is but a construction which the mind has made from some few among the wealth of materials at its disposal.

The relation of this universe to the world of fact is not unlike the relation between a tapestry picture and the scene which it imitates. You, practical man, are obliged to weave your image of the outer world upon the hard warp of your own mentality, which perpetually imposes its own convention, and checks the free representation of life. As a tapestry picture, however various and full of meaning, is ultimately reducible to little squares, so the world of common sense is ultimately reducible to a series of static elements conditioned by the machinery of the brain. Subtle curves, swift movement, delicate gradation, that machinery cannot represent. It leaves them out. From the countless suggestions, the tangle of many-colored wools which the real world presents to you, you snatch one here and there. Of these you weave together those which are the most useful, the most obvious, the most often repeated: which make a tidy and coherent pattern when seen on the right side. Shut up with this symbolic picture, you soon drop into the habit of behaving to it as though it were not a representation but a thing. On it you fix your attention; with it you "unite." Yet, did you look at the wrong side, at the many short ends, the clumsy joins and patches, this simple philosophy might be disturbed. You would be forced to acknowledge the conventional character of the picture you have made so cleverly, the wholesale waste of material involved in the weaving of it: for only a few among the wealth of impressions we receive are seized and incorporated into our picture of the world. Further, it might occur to you that a slight alteration in the rhythm of the senses would place at your disposal a complete new range of material, opening your eyes and ears to sounds, colors, and movements now inaudible and invisible, removing from your universe those which you now regard as part of the established order of things. Even the strands which you have made use of might have been combined in some other way, with disastrous results to the "world of common sense," yet without any diminution of their own reality.

Nor can you regard these strands themselves as ultimate. As the most prudent of logicians might venture to deduce from a skein of wool the probable existence of a sheep, so you, from the raw stuff of perception, may venture to deduce a universe which transcends the reproductive powers of your loom. Even the camera of the photographer, more apt at contemplation than the mind of man, has shown us how limited are these powers in some directions, and enlightened us as to a few of the cruder errors of the person who accepts its products at face value, or, as he would say, believes his own eyes. It has shown us, for instance, that the galloping racehorse, with legs stretched out as we are used to see it, is a mythical animal, probably founded on the mental image of a running dog. No horse has ever galloped thus: but its real action is too quick for us, and we explain it to ourselves as something resembling the more deliberate dog action which we have caught and registered as it passed. The plain man's universe is full of racehorses which are really running dogs; of conventional waves, first seen in pictures and then imagined upon the sea; of psychological situations taken from books and applied to human life; of racial peculiarities generalized from insufficient data, and then "discovered" in actuality; of theological

diagrams and scientific "laws," flung upon the background of eternity as the magic lantern's image is
reflected on the screen.

The colored scene at which you look so trustfully
owes, in fact, much of its character to the activities of
the seer: to that process of thought—concept—cogi-
tation, from which Keats prayed with so great an
ardor to escape, when he exclaimed in words which
will seem to you, according to the temper of your
mind, either an invitation to the higher laziness or
one of the most profound aspirations of the soul,
"O for a life of sensations rather than thoughts!"
He felt—as all the poets have felt with him—that
another, lovelier world, tinted with unimaginable
wonders, alive with ultimate music, awaited those
who could free themselves from the fetters of the
mind, lay down the shuttle and the weaver's comb,
and reach out beyond the conceptual image to intuitive contact with the Thing.

There are certain happy accidents which have the
power of inducting man for a moment into this
richer and more vital world. These stop, as one old
mystic said, the "wheel of his imagination," the
dreadful energy of his image-making power weaving up and transmuting the incoming messages of
sense. They snatch him from the loom and place
him, in the naked simplicity of his spirit, face-to-face
with that Other than himself whence the materials
of his industry have come. In these hours human
consciousness ascends from thought to contemplation; becomes at least aware of the world in which
the mystics dwell; and perceives for an instant, as St.

Augustine did, "the light that never changes, above the eye of the soul, above the intelligence." This experience might be called in essence "absolute sensation." It is a pure feeling-state, in which the fragmentary contacts with Reality achieved through the senses are merged in a wholeness of communion which feels and knows all at once, yet in a way which the reason can never understand, that Totality of which fragments are known by the lover, the musician, and the artist.

If the doors of perception were cleansed, said Blake, everything would appear to man as it is—Infinite.[6] But the doors of perception are hung with the cobwebs of thought: prejudice, cowardice, sloth. Eternity is with us, inviting our contemplation perpetually, but we are too frightened, lazy, and suspicious to respond: too arrogant to still our thought, and let divine sensation have its way. It needs industry and goodwill if we would make that transition: for the process involves a veritable spring cleaning of the soul, a turning out and rearrangement of our mental furniture, a wide opening of closed windows, that the notes of the wild birds beyond our garden may come to us fully charged with wonder and freshness, and drown with their music the noise of the gramophone within. Those who do this discover that they have lived in a stuffy world, while their inheritance was a world of morning glory, where every titmouse is a celestial messenger, and

---

6. See epigraph on page v of this volume. (Eds.)

every thrusting bud is charged with the full significance of life.

There will be many who feel a certain skepticism
as to the possibility of the undertaking here suggested to them, a prudent unwillingness to sacrifice
their old comfortably upholstered universe, on the
mere promise that they will receive a new heaven
and a new earth in exchange. These careful ones
may like to remind themselves that the vision of the
world presented to us by all the great artists and
poets—those creatures whose very existence would
seem so strange to us, were we not accustomed to
them—perpetually demonstrates the many-graded
character of human consciousness; the new worlds
which await it, once it frees itself from the tyranny
of those labor-saving contrivances with which it
usually works. Leaving on one side the more subtle
apprehensions which we call "spiritual," even the
pictures of the old Chinese draftsmen and the modern impressionists, of Watteau and of Turner, of
Manet, Degas, and Cézanne; the poems of Blake,
Wordsworth, Shelley, Whitman—these, and countless others, assure you that their creators have enjoyed
direct communion, not with some vague world of
fancy, but with a visible natural order which you
have never known. These have seized and woven
into their pictures strands which never presented
themselves to you; significant forms which elude
you, tones and relations to which you are blind, living facts for which your conventional world provides no place. They prove by their works that
Blake was right when he said that "a fool sees not

the same tree that a wise man sees"; and that psychologists, insisting on the selective action of the mind, the fact that our preconceptions govern the character of our universe, do but teach the most demonstrable of truths. Did you take them seriously, as you should, their ardent reports might well disgust you with the dull and narrow character of your own consciousness.

What is it, then, which distinguishes the outlook of great poets and artists from the arrogant subjectivism of common sense? Innocence and humility distinguish it. These persons prejudge nothing, criticize nothing. To some extent, their attitude to the universe is that of children: and because this is so, they participate to that extent in the Heaven of Reality. According to their measure, they have fulfilled Keats's aspiration, they do live a life in which the emphasis lies on sensation rather than on thought: for the state which he then struggled to describe was that ideal state of pure receptivity, of perfect correspondence with the essence of things, of which all artists have a share, and which a few great mystics appear to have possessed—not indeed in its entirety, but to an extent which made them, as they say, "one with the Reality of things." The greater the artist is, the wider and deeper is the range of this pure sensation: the more sharply he is aware of the torrent of life and loveliness, the rich profusion of possible beauties and shapes. He always wants to press deeper and deeper, to let the span of his perception spread wider and wider, till he unites with the whole of that Reality which he feels all about him, and of which his own life is a part. He is always tending, in fact, to pass over from the artistic to the mystical state. In artistic experience, then, in the artist's perennial effort to actualize the ideal which Keats expressed, we may find a point of departure for our exploration of the contemplative life.

What would it mean for a soul that truly captured it, this life in which the emphasis should lie on the immediate percepts, the messages the world pours in on us, instead of on the sophisticated universe into which our clever brains transmute them? Plainly, it would mean the achievement of a new universe, a new order of reality: escape from the terrible museumlike world of daily life, where everything is classified and labeled, and all the graded fluid facts which have no label are ignored. It would mean an innocence of eye and innocence of ear impossible for us to conceive; the impassioned contemplation of pure form, freed from all the meanings with which the mind has draped and disguised it; the recapturing of the lost mysteries of touch and fragrance, most wonderful among the avenues of sense. It would mean the exchanging of the neat conceptual world our thoughts build up, fenced in by the solid ramparts of the possible, for the inconceivable richness of that unwalled world from which we have subtracted it. It would mean that we should receive from every flower, not merely a beautiful image to which the label "flower" has been affixed, but the full impact of its unimaginable beauty and wonder, the direct sensation of life having communion with life: that the scents of ceasing rain, the voice of trees, the deep softness of the kitten's fur, the acrid touch of sorrel on the tongue should be in themselves profound, complete, and simple experiences, calling forth simplicity of response in our souls.

Thus understood, the life of pure sensation is the meat and drink of poetry, and one of the most accessible avenues to that union with Reality which the mystic declares to us as the very object of life. But the poet must take that living stuff direct from the field and river, without sophistication, without criticism, as the life of the soul is taken direct from the altar, with an awe that admits not of analysis. He must not subject it to the cooking, filtering process of the brain. It is because he knows how to elude this dreadful sophistication of Reality, because his attitude to the universe is governed by the supreme artistic virtues of humility and love, that poetry is what it is: and I include in the sweep of poetic art the colored poetry of the painter, and the wordless poetry of the musician and the dancer too.

At this point the critical reader will certainly offer an objection. "You have been inviting me," he will say, "to do nothing more or less than trust my senses: and this too on the authority of those impracticable dreamers, the poets. Now it is notorious that our senses deceive us. Everyone knows that; and even your own remarks have already suggested it. How, then, can a wholesale and uncritical acceptance of my sensations help me to unite with Reality? Many of these sensations we share with the animals: in some, the animals obviously surpass us. Will you suggest that my terrier, smelling his way through an uncoordinated universe, is a better mystic than I?"

To this I reply that the terrier's contacts with the world are doubtless crude and imperfect; yet he has indeed preserved a directness of apprehension which you have lost. He gets, and responds to, the real smell, not a notion or a name. Certainly the senses, when taken at face value, do deceive us: yet the deception resides not so much in them, as in that conceptual world which we insist on building up from their reports, and for which we make them responsible. They deceive us less when we receive these reports uncooked and unclassified, as simple and direct experiences. Then, behind the special and imperfect stammerings which we call color, sound, fragrance, and the rest, we sometimes discern a *whole fact*—at once divinely simple and infinitely various—from which these partial messages proceed, and which seeks as it were to utter itself in them. And we feel, when this is so, that the fact thus glimpsed is of an immense significance, imparting to that aspect of the world which we are able to perceive all the significance, all the character which it possesses. The more of the artist there is in us, the more intense that significance, that character, will seem: the more complete, too, will be our conviction that our uneasiness, the vagueness of our reactions to things, would be cured could we reach and unite with the fact, instead of our notion of it. And it is just such an act of union, reached through the clarified channels of sense and unadulterated by the content of thought, which the great artist or poet achieves.

We seem in these words to have come far from the mystic, and that contemplative consciousness wherewith he ascends to the contact of Truth. As a matter of fact, we are merely considering that consciousness in its most natural and accessible form: for contemplation is, on the one hand, the essential activity of all artists; on the other, the art through which those who choose to learn and practice it may share in some fragmentary degree, according to their measure, the special experience of the mystic and the poet. By it they may achieve that virginal outlook upon things, that celestial power of communion with veritable life, which comes when that which we call "sensation" is freed from the tyranny of that which we call "thought." The artist is no more and no less than a contemplative who has learned to express himself, and who tells his love in color, speech, or sound: the mystic, upon one side of his nature, is an artist of a special and exalted kind, who tries to express something of the revelation he has received, mediates between Reality and the race. In the game of give and take which goes on between the human consciousness and the external world, both have learned to put the emphasis upon the message from without, rather than on their own reaction to and rearrangement of it. Both have exchanged the false imagination which draws the sensations and intuitions of the self into its own narrow circle, and there distorts and transforms them, for the true imagination which pours itself out, eager, adventurous, and self-giving, toward the greater universe.

Chapter III

THE PREPARATION OF THE MYSTIC

Here the practical man will naturally say: And pray how am I going to do this? How shall I detach myself from the artificial world to which I am accustomed? Where is the brake that shall stop the wheel of my image-making mind?

I answer: You are going to do it by an education process; a drill, of which the first stages will, indeed, be hard enough. You have already acknowledged the need of such mental drill, such deliberate selective acts, in respect to the smaller matters of life. You willingly spend time and money over that narrowing and sharpening of attention which you call a "business training," a "legal education," the "acquirement of a scientific method." But this new undertaking will involve the development and the training of a layer of your consciousness which has lain fallow in the past; the acquirement of a method you have never used before. It is reasonable, even reassuring, that hard work and discipline should be needed for this: that it should demand of you, if not the renunciation of the cloister, at least the virtues of the golf course.

The education of the mystical sense begins in self-simplification. The feeling, willing, seeing self is to move from the various and the analytic to the simple and the synthetic: a sentence which may cause hard breathing and mopping of the brows on the part of the practical man. Yet it is to you, practical man, reading these pages as you rush through the Tube[7] to the practical work of rearranging unimportant fragments of your universe, that this message so needed by your time—or rather, by your want of time—is addressed. To you, unconscious analyst, so busy reading the advertisements upon the carriage wall that you hardly observe the stages of your unceasing flight: so anxiously acquisitive of the crumbs that you never lift your eyes to the loaf. The essence of mystical contemplation is summed in these two experiences—union with the flux of life, and union with the Whole in which all lesser realities are resumed—and these experiences are well within your reach. Though it is likely that the accusation will annoy you, you are already in fact a potential contemplative: for this act, as St. Thomas Aquinas taught, is proper to all men—is, indeed, the characteristic human activity.

More, it is probable that you are, or have been, an actual contemplative too. Has it never happened to you to lose yourself for a moment in a swift and satisfying experience for which you found no name? When the world took on a strangeness, and you rushed out to meet it, in a mood at once exultant and ashamed? Was there not an instant when you took the lady who now orders your dinner into your

---

7. I.e., the London Underground. (Eds.)

arms, and she suddenly interpreted to you the whole of the universe?—a universe so great, charged with so terrible an intensity, that you have hardly dared to think of it since. Do you remember that horrid moment at the concert, when you became wholly unaware of your comfortable seven-and-sixpenny seat? Those were onsets of involuntary contemplation, sudden partings of the conceptual veil. Dare you call them the least significant moments of your life? Did you not then, like the African saint, "thrill with love and dread," though you were not provided with a label for that which you adored?

It will not help you to speak of these experiences as "mere emotion." Mere emotion then inducted you into a world which you recognized as more valid—in the highest sense, more rational—than that in which you usually dwell: a world which had a wholeness, a meaning, which exceeded the sum of its parts. Mere emotion then brought you to your knees, made you at once proud and humble, showed you your place. It simplified and unified existence: it stripped off the little accidents and ornaments which perpetually deflect our vagrant attention, and gathered up the whole being of you into one state, which felt and knew a Reality that your intelligence could not comprehend. Such an emotion is the driving power of spirit, an august and ultimate thing: and this your innermost inhabitant felt it to be, while your eyes were open to the light.

Now that simplifying act, which is the preliminary of all mystical experience, that gathering of the scattered bits of personality into the *one* which is really you—into the "unity of your spirit," as the mystics say—the great forces of love, beauty, wonder, grief may do for you now and again. These lift you perforce from the consideration of the details to the contemplation of the All: turn you from the tidy world of image to the ineffable world of fact. But they are fleeting and ungovernable experiences, descending with dreadful violence on the soul. Are you willing that your participation in Reality shall depend wholly on these incalculable visitations: on the sudden wind and rain that wash your windows, and let in the vision of the landscape at your gates? You can, if you like, keep those windows clear. You can, if you choose to turn your attention that way, learn to look out of them. These are the two great phases in the education of every contemplative: and they are called in the language of the mystics the purification of the senses and the purification of the will.

Those who are so fortunate as to experience in one of its many forms the crisis which is called "conversion" are seized, as it seems to them, by some power stronger than themselves and turned perforce in the right direction. They find that this irresistible power has cleansed the windows of their homely coat of grime; and they look out, literally, upon a new heaven and new earth. The long quiet work of adjustment which others must undertake before any certitude rewards them is for these concentrated into one violent shattering and rearranging of the self, which can now begin its true career of correspondence with the Reality it has perceived. To persons of this type I do not address myself, but rather to the ordinary plodding scholar of life, who must reach the same goal by a more gradual road.

What is it that smears the windows of the senses? Thought, convention, self-interest. We throw a mist of thought between ourselves and the external world: and through this we discern, as in a glass darkly, that which we have arranged to see. We see it in the way in which our neighbors see it; sometimes through a pink veil, sometimes through a gray. Religion, indigestion, priggishness, or discontent may drape the panes. The prismatic colors of a fashionable school of art may stain them. Inevitably, too, we see the narrow world our windows show us, not "in itself," but in relation to our own needs, moods, and preferences, which exercise a selective control upon those few aspects of the whole which penetrate to the field of consciousness and dictate the order in which we arrange them, for the universe of the natural man is strictly egocentric. We continue to name the living creatures with all the placid assurance of Adam: and whatsoever we call them, that is the name thereof. Unless we happen to be artists—and then but rarely—we never know the "thing seen" in its purity; never, from birth to death, look at it with disinterested eyes. Our vision and understanding of it are governed by all that we bring with us, and mix with it, to form an amalgam with which the mind can deal. To "purify" the senses is to release them, so far as human beings may, from the tyranny of egocentric judgments; to make of them the organs of direct perception. This means that we must crush our deep-seated passion for classification and correspondences; ignore the instinctive, selfish question, "What does it mean to *me?*"; learn to dip ourselves in the universe at our gates, and know it, not from without by comprehension, but from within by self-mergence.

Richard of St. Victor[8] has said that the essence of all purification is self-simplification, the doing away of the unnecessary and unreal, the tangles and complications of consciousness: and we must remember that when these masters of the spiritual life speak of purity, they have in their minds no thin, abstract notion of a rule of conduct stripped of all color and compounded chiefly of refusals, such as a more modern, more arid asceticism set up. Their purity is an affirmative state; something strong, clean, and crystalline, capable of a wholeness of adjustment to the wholeness of a God-inhabited world. The pure soul is like a lens from which all irrelevancies and excrescences, all the beams and motes of egotism and prejudice, have been removed, so that it may reflect a clear image of the one Transcendent Fact within which all other facts are held.

> *All which I took from thee I did but take,*
> *Not for thy harms,*
> *But just that thou might'st seek it in My arms.*[9]

---

8. Mystic writer and Augustinian monk (d. 1173). (Eds.)

9. From "The Hound of Heaven," by Francis Thompson, English Roman Catholic poet (1859–1907). (Eds.)

All the details of existence, all satisfactions of the heart and mind, are resumed within that Transcendent Fact as all the colors of the spectrum are included in white light: and we possess them best by passing beyond them, by following back the many to the One.

The "Simple Eye" of Contemplation, about which the mystic writers say so much, is then a synthetic sense which sees that white light in which all color is, without discrete analysis of its properties. The Simple Ear which discerns the celestial melody hears that Tone in which all music is resumed, thus achieving that ecstatic life of "sensation without thought" which Keats perceived to be the substance of true happiness.

But you, practical man, have lived all your days among the illusions of multiplicity. Though you are using at every instant your innate tendency to synthesis and simplification, since this alone creates the semblance of order in your universe—though what you call seeing and hearing are themselves great unifying acts—yet your attention to life has been deliberately adjusted to a world of frittered values and prismatic refracted lights: full of incompatible interests, of people, principles, things. Ambitions and affections, tastes and prejudices, are fighting for your attention. Your poor, worried consciousness flies to and fro among them; it has become a restless and a complicated thing. At this very moment your thoughts are buzzing like a swarm of bees. The reduction of this fevered complex to a unity appears to be a task beyond all human power. Yet the situation is not as hopeless for you as it seems. All this is only happening upon the periphery of the mind, where it touches and reacts to the world of appearance. At the center there is a stillness which even you are not able to break. There, the rhythm of your duration is one with the rhythm of the Universal Life. There, your essential self exists: the permanent being which persists through and behind the flow and change of your conscious states. You have been snatched to that center once or twice. Turn your consciousness inward to it deliberately. Retreat to that point whence all the various lines of your activities flow, and to which at last they must return. Since this alone of all that you call your "selfhood" is possessed of Eternal Reality, it is surely a counsel of prudence to acquaint yourself with its peculiarities and its powers. "Take your seat within the heart of the thousand-petaled lotus," cries the Eastern visionary. "Hold thou to thy Center," says his Christian brother, "and all things shall be thine." This is a practical recipe, not a pious exhortation. The thing may sound absurd to you, but you can do it if you will: standing back, as it were, from the vague and purposeless reactions in which most men fritter their vital energies. Then you can survey with a certain calm, a certain detachment, your universe and the possibilities of life within it: can discern too, if you be at all inclined to mystical adventure, the stages of the road along which you must pass on your way toward harmony with the Real.

This universe, these possibilities, are far richer,

yet far simpler than you have supposed. Seen from the true center of personality, instead of the usual angle of self-interest, their scattered parts arrange themselves in order: you begin to perceive those graduated levels of Reality with which a purified and intensified consciousness can unite. So, too, the road is more logically planned, falls into more comprehensible stages, than those who dwell in a world of single vision are willing to believe.

Now it is a paradox of human life, often observed even by the most concrete and unimaginative of philosophers, that man seems to be poised between two contradictory orders of Reality. Two planes of existence—or, perhaps, two ways of apprehending existence—lie within the possible span of his consciousness. That great pair of opposites which metaphysicians call Being and Becoming, Eternity and Time, Unity and Multiplicity, and others mean, when they speak of the Spiritual and the Natural Worlds, represents the two extreme forms under which the universe can be realized by him. The greatest men, those whose consciousness is extended to full span, can grasp, be aware of, both. They know themselves to live, both in the discrete, manifested, ever-changeful parts and appearances, and also in the Whole Fact. They react fully to both: for them there is no conflict between the parochial and the patriotic sense. More than this, a deep instinct sometimes assures them that the inner spring or secret of that Whole Fact is also the inner spring and secret of their individual lives: and that here, in this third factor, the disharmonies between the part and the whole are resolved. As they know themselves to dwell in the world of time and yet to be capable of transcending it, so the Ultimate Reality, they think, inhabits yet inconceivably exceeds all that they know to be—as the soul of the musician controls and exceeds not merely each note of the flowing melody, but also the whole of that symphony in which these cadences must play their part. That invulnerable spark of vivid life, that "inward light" which these men find at their own centers when they seek for it, is for them an earnest of the Uncreated Light, the ineffable splendor of God, dwelling at, and energizing within, the heart of things: for this spark is at once one with, yet separate from, the Universal Soul.

So then, man, in the person of his greatest and most living representatives, feels himself to have implicit correspondences with three levels of existence, which we may call the Natural, the Spiritual, and the Divine. The road on which he is to travel therefore, the mystical education which he is to undertake, shall successively unite him with these three worlds, stretching his consciousness to the point at which he finds them first as three, and at last as One. Under normal circumstances even the first of them, the natural world of Becoming, is only present to him—unless he be an artist—in a vague and fragmentary way. He is, of course, aware of the temporal order, a ceaseless change and movement, birth, growth, and death, of which he is a part. But the rapture and splendor of that everlasting flux which India calls the Sport of God hardly reaches his understanding; he is too busy with his own little movements to feel the full current of the stream.

But under those abnormal circumstances on which we have touched, a deeper level of his consciousness comes into focus; he hears the music of surrounding things. Then he rises, through and with his aware-ness of the great life of Nature, to the knowledge that he is part of another greater life, transcending succession. In this his durational spirit is immersed. Here all the highest values of existence are stored for him: and it is because of his existence within this Eternal Reality, his patriotic relationship to it, that the efforts and experiences of the time-world have significance for him. It is from the vantage point gained when he realizes his contacts with this higher order that he can see with the clear eye of the artist or the mystic the World of Becoming itself—recog-nize its proportions—even reach out to some faint intuition of its ultimate worth. So, if he would be a whole man, if he would realize all that is implicit in his humanity, he must actualize his relationship with this supernal plane of Being: and he shall do it, as we have seen, by simplification, by a deliberate withdrawal of attention from the bewildering mul-tiplicity of things, a deliberate humble surrender of his image-making consciousness. He already pos-sesses, at that gathering point of personality which the old writers sometimes called the "apex" and sometimes the "ground" of the soul, a medium of

communication with Reality. But this spiritual principle, this gathering point of his selfhood, is just that
aspect of him which is furthest removed from the
active surface consciousness. He treats it as the busy
citizen treats his national monuments. It is there, it
is important, a possession which adds dignity to his
existence; but he never has time to go in. Yet as the
purified sense, cleansed of prejudice and self-interest,
can give us fleeting communications from the actual
broken-up world of duration at our gates: so the
purified and educated will can wholly withdraw the
self's attention from its usual concentration on small
useful aspects of the time-world, refuse to react to its
perpetually incoming messages, retreat to the unity
of its spirit, and there make itself ready for messages
from another plane. This is the process which the
mystics call Recollection: the first stage in the training of the contemplative consciousness.

We begin, therefore, to see that the task of union
with Reality will involve certain stages of preparation as well as stages of attainment; and these stages
of preparation—for some disinterested souls easy
and rapid, for others long and full of pain—may be
grouped under two heads. First, the disciplining and
simplifying of the attention, which is the essence of
Recollection. Next, the disciplining and simplifying
of the affections and will, the orientation of the
heart; which is sometimes called by the formidable
name of Purgation. So the practical mysticism of the
plain man will best be grasped by him as a fivefold
scheme of training and growth: in which the first

two stages prepare the self for union with Reality, and the last three unite it successively with the World of Becoming, the World of Being, and finally with that Ultimate Fact which the philosopher calls the Absolute and the religious mystic calls God.

Chapter IV

MEDITATION AND RECOLLECTION

Recollection, the art which the practical man is now invited to learn, is in essence no more and no less than the subjection of the attention to the control of the will. It is not, therefore, a purely mystical activity. In one form or another it is demanded of all who would get control of their own mental processes, and does or should represent the first great step in the education of the human consciousness. So slothful, however, is man in all that concerns his higher faculties, that few deliberately undertake this education at all. They are content to make their contacts with things by a vague, unregulated power, ever apt to play truant, ever apt to fail them. Unless they be spurred to it by that passion for ultimate things which expresses itself in religion, philosophy, or art, they seldom learn the secret of a voluntary concentration of the mind.

Since the philosopher's interests are mainly objective, and the artist seldom cogitates on his own processes, it is, in the end, to the initiate of religion that we are forced to go, if we would learn how to undertake this training for ourselves. The religious contemplative has this further attraction for us: that he is by nature a missionary as well. The vision which he has achieved is the vision of an intensely loving heart; and love, which cannot keep itself to itself, urges him to tell the news as widely and as clearly as he may. In his works, he is ever trying to reveal the secret of his own deeper life and wider vision, and to help his fellow men to share it: hence he provides the clearest, most orderly, most practical teachings on the art of contemplation that we are likely to find. True, our purpose in attempting this art may seem to us very different from his: though if we carry out the principles involved to their last term, we shall probably find that they have brought us to the place at which he aimed from the first. But the method, in its earlier stages, must be the same, whether we call the Reality which is the object of our quest aesthetic, cosmic, or divine. The athlete must develop much the same muscles, endure much the same discipline, whatever be the game he means to play.

So we will go straight to St. Teresa, and inquire of her what was the method by which she taught her daughters to gather themselves together, to capture and hold the attitude most favorable to communion with the spiritual world. She tells us—and here she accords with the great tradition of the Christian contemplatives, a tradition which was evolved under the pressure of long experience—that the process is a gradual one. The method to be employed is a slow, patient training of material which the license of years has made intractable, not the sudden easy turning of the mind in a new direction, that it may minister to a new fancy for "the mystical view of things." Recollection begins, she says, in the deliberate and regular practice of meditation, a perfectly natural form of mental exercise, though at first a hard one.

Now meditation is a halfway house between think-ing and contemplating: and as a discipline, it derives its chief value from this transitional character. The real mystical life, which is the truly practical life, begins at the beginning; not with supernatural acts and ecstatic apprehensions, but with the normal fac-ulties of the normal man. "I do not require of you," says Teresa to her pupils in meditation, "to form great and curious considerations in your under-standing: I require of you no more than to *look*."

It might be thought that such looking at the spiri-tual world, simply, intensely, without cleverness—such an opening of the Eye of Eternity—was the essence of contemplation itself: and indeed one of the best definitions has described that art as a "lov-ing sight," a "peering into heaven with the ghostly eye." But the self who is yet at this early stage of the pathway to Reality is not asked to look at anything new, to peer into the deeps of things: only to gaze with a new and cleansed vision on the ordinary intellectual images, the labels and the formulae, the "objects" and ideas—even the external symbols—among which it has always dwelled. It is not yet advanced to the seeing of fresh landscapes: it is only able to reexamine the furniture of its home, and obtain from this exercise a skill, and a control of the attention, which shall afterward be applied to greater purposes. Its task is here to *consider* that furniture, as the Victorines called this preliminary training: to take, that is, a more starry view of it: standing back from the whirl of the earth, and observing the process of things.

Take, then, an idea, an object, from among the common stock, and hold it before your mind. The selection is large enough: all sentient beings may find subjects of meditation to their taste, for there lies a universal behind every particular of thought, however concrete it may appear, and within the most rational propositions the meditative eye may glimpse a dream.

> *Reason has moons, but moons not hers*
> *Lie mirror'd on her sea,*
> *Confounding her astronomers*
> *But, O delighting me.*[10]

Even those objects which minister to our sense-life may well be used to nourish our spirits too. Who has not watched the intent meditations of a comfortable cat brooding upon the Absolute Mouse? You, if you have a philosophic twist, may transcend such relative views of Reality, and try to meditate on Time, Succession, even Being itself: or again on human intercourse, birth, growth, and death, on a flower, a river, the various tapestries of the sky. Even your own emotional life will provide you with the ideas of love, joy, peace, mercy, conflict, desire. You may range, with Kant, from the stars to the moral law. If your turn be to religion, the richest and most evoca-

---

10. By Ralph Hodgson (1872–1962), English poet. (Eds.)

tive of fields is open to your choice: from the plaster image to the mysteries of Faith.

But, the choice made, it must be held and defended during the time of meditation against all invasions from without, however insidious their encroachments, however "spiritual" their disguise. It must be brooded upon, gazed at, seized again and again, as distractions seem to snatch it from your grasp. A restless boredom, a dreary conviction of your own incapacity, will presently attack you. This, too, must be resisted at swordpoint. The first quarter of an hour thus spent in attempted meditation will be, indeed, a time of warfare; which should at least convince you how unruly, how ill-educated is your attention, how miserably ineffective your will, how far away you are from the captaincy of your own soul. It should convince, too, the most commonsense of philosophers of the distinction between real time, the true stream of duration which is life, and the sequence of seconds so carefully measured by the clock. Never before has the stream flowed so slowly, or fifteen minutes taken so long to pass. Consciousness has been lifted to a longer, slower rhythm, and is not yet adjusted to its solemn march.

But, striving for this new poise, intent on the achievement of it, presently it will happen to you to find that you have indeed—though how you know not—entered upon a fresh plane of perception, altered your relation with things.

First, the subject of your meditation begins, as you surrender to its influence, to exhibit unsuspected meaning, beauty, power. A perpetual growth

of significance keeps pace with the increase of attention which you bring to bear on it; that attention
which is the one agent of all your apprehensions,
physical and mental alike. It ceases to be thin and
abstract. You sink as it were into the deeps of it, rest
in it, "unite" with it; and learn, in this still, intent
communion, something of its depth and breadth
and height, as we learn by direct intercourse to
know our friends.

Moreover, as your meditation becomes deeper it
will defend you from the perpetual assaults of the
outer world. You will hear the busy hum of that
world as a distant exterior melody, and know yourself to be in some sort withdrawn from it. You have
set a ring of silence between you and it; and behold!
within that silence you are free. You will look at the
colored scene, and it will seem to you thin and
papery: only one among countless possible images of
a deeper life as yet beyond your reach. And gradually, you will come to be aware of an entity, a *You,*
who can thus hold at arm's length, be aware of, look
at, an idea—a universe—other than itself. By this
voluntary painful act of concentration, this first step
upon the ladder which goes—as the mystics would
say—from "multiplicity to unity," you have to some
extent withdrawn yourself from that union with
unrealities, with notions and concepts, which has
hitherto contented you; and at once all the values
of existence are changed. "The road to a Yea lies
through a Nay." You, in this preliminary movement
of recollection, are saying your first deliberate No to
the claim which the world of appearance makes to a

total possession of your consciousness: and are thus making possible some contact between that consciousness and the World of Reality.

Now turn this new purified and universalized gaze back upon yourself. Observe your own being in a fresh relation with things, and surrender yourself willingly to the moods of astonishment, humility, joy—perhaps of deep shame or sudden love—which invade your heart as you look. So doing patiently, day after day, constantly recapturing the vagrant attention, ever renewing the struggle for simplicity of sight, you will at last discover that there is something within you—something behind the fractious, conflicting life of desire—which you can recollect, gather up, make effective for new life. You will, in fact, know your own soul for the first time, and learn that there is a sense in which this real *You* is distinct from, an alien within, the world in which you find yourself, as an actor has another life when he is not on the stage. When you do not merely believe this but know it; when you have achieved this power of withdrawing yourself, of making this first crude distinction between appearance and reality, the initial stage of the contemplative life has been won. It is not much more of an achievement than that first proud effort in which the baby stands upright for a moment and then relapses to the more natural and convenient crawl: but it holds within it the same earnest of future development.

Chapter V
SELF-ADJUSTMENT

So, in a measure, you have found yourself: have retreated behind all that flowing appearance, that busy, unstable consciousness with its moods and obsessions, its feverish alternations of interest and apathy, its conflicts and irrational impulses, which even the psychologists mistake for You. Thanks to this recollective act, you have discovered in your inmost sanctuary a being not wholly practical, who refuses to be satisfied by your busy life of correspondences with the world of normal men, and hungers for communion with a spiritual universe. And this thing so foreign to your surface consciousness, yet familiar to it and continuous with it, you recognize as the true Self whose existence you always took for granted, but whom you have only known hitherto in its scattered manifestations. "That art thou."

This climb up the mountain of self-knowledge, said the Victorine mystics, is the necessary prelude to all illumination. Only at its summit do we discover, as Dante did, the beginning of the pathway to Reality. It is a lonely and an arduous excursion, a sufficient test of courage and sincerity: for most men prefer to dwell in comfortable ignorance upon the lower slopes, and there to make of their more obvious characteristics a drapery which shall veil the naked truth. True and complete self-knowledge, indeed, is the privilege of the strongest alone. Few can bear to contemplate themselves face-to-face; for the vision is strange and terrible, and brings awe and contrition in its wake. The life of the seer is changed by it forever. He is converted, in the deepest and most drastic sense; is forced to take up a new attitude toward himself and all other things. Likely enough, if you really knew yourself—saw your own dim character, perpetually at the mercy of its environment; your true motives, stripped for inspection and measured against eternal values; your unacknowledged self-indulgences; your irrational loves and hates—you would be compelled to remodel your whole existence, and become for the first time a practical man.

But you have done what you can in this direction; have at last discovered your own deeper being, your eternal spark, the agent of all your contacts with Reality. You have often read about it. Now you have met it; know for a fact that it is there. What next? What changes, what readjustments will this self-revelation involve for you?

You will have noticed, as with practice your familiarity with the state of Recollection has increased, that the kind of consciousness which it brings with it, the sort of attitude which it demands of you, conflict sharply with the consciousness and the attitude which you have found so appropriate to your ordinary life in the past. They make this old attitude appear childish, unworthy, at last absurd. By this first deliberate effort to attend to Reality you are at once brought face-to-face with that dreadful revelation of disharmony, unrealness, and interior muddle which the blunt moralists call "conviction of sin." Never again need those moralists point out to you the inherent silliness of your earnest pursuit of impermanent things: your solemn concentration upon the game of getting on. Nonetheless, this attitude persists. Again and again you swing back to it. Something more than realization is needed if you are to adjust yourself to your new vision of the world. This game which you have played so long has formed and conditioned you, developing certain qualities and perceptions, leaving the rest in abeyance: so that now, suddenly asked to play another, which demands fresh movements, alertness of a different sort, your mental muscles are intractable, your attention refuses to respond. Nothing less will serve you here than that drastic remodeling of character which the mystics called "Purgation," the second stage in the training of the human consciousness for participation in Reality.

It is not merely that your intellect has assimilated, united with a superficial and unreal view of the world. Far worse: your will, your desire, the sum total of your energy, has been turned the wrong way, harnessed to the wrong machine. You have become accustomed to the idea that you want, or ought to want, certain valueless things, certain specific positions. For years your treasure has been in the Stock Exchange, or the House of Commons, or the Salon, or the reviews that "really count" (if they still exist), or the drawing rooms of Mayfair; and thither your heart perpetually tends to stray. Habit has you in its chains. You are not free. The awakening, then, of your deeper self, which knows not habit and desires nothing but free correspondence with the Real, awakens you at once to the fact of a disharmony between the simple but inexorable longings and instincts of the buried spirit, now beginning to assert themselves in your hours of meditation—pushing out, as it were, toward the light—and the various changeful but insistent longings and instincts of the surface-self. Between these two no peace is possible: they conflict at every turn. It becomes apparent to you that the declaration of Plotinus, accepted or repeated by all the mystics, concerning a "higher" and a "lower" life, and the cleavage that exists between them, has a certain justification even in the experience of the ordinary man.

That great thinker and ecstatic said that all human personality was thus twofold: thus capable of correspondence with two orders of existence. The "higher life" was always tending toward union with Reality, toward the gathering of itself up into One. The "lower life," framed for correspondence with the outward world of multiplicity, was always tending to fall downward, and fritter the powers of the self among external things. This is but a restatement, in terms of practical existence, of the fact which Recollection brought home to us: that the human self is transitional, neither angel nor animal, capable of living toward either Eternity or Time. But it is one thing to frame beautiful theories on these subjects, another when the unresolved dualism of your own personality (though you may not give it this high-sounding name) becomes the main fact of consciousness, perpetually reasserts itself as a vital problem, and refuses to take academic rank.

This state of things means the acute discomfort which ensues on being pulled two ways at once. The uneasy swaying of attention between two incompatible ideals, the alternating conviction that there is something wrong, perverse, poisonous, about life as you have always lived it, and something hopelessly ethereal about the life which your innermost inhabitant wants to live—these disagreeable sensations grow stronger and stronger. First one and then the other asserts itself. You fluctuate miserably between their attractions and their claims, and will have no peace until these claims have been met, and the apparent opposition between them resolved. You are sure now that there is another, more durable and more "reasonable," life possible to the human consciousness than that on which it usually spends itself. But it is also clear to you that you must yourself be something more, or other, than you are now, if you are to achieve this life, dwell in it, and breathe its air. You have had in your brief spells of recollection a first quick vision of that plane of being which Augustine called "the land of peace," the "beauty old and new." You know forevermore that it exists: that the real thing within yourself belongs to it, might live in it, is being all the time invited and enticed to it. You begin, in fact, to feel and know in every fiber of your being the mystical need of "union with Reality" and to realize that the natural scene which you have accepted so trustfully cannot provide the correspondences toward which you are stretching out.

Nevertheless, it is to correspondences with this natural order that you have given for many years your full attention, your desire, your will. The surface-self, left for so long in undisputed possession of the conscious field, has grown strong, and cemented itself like a limpet to the rock of the obvious, gladly exchanging freedom for apparent security, and building up, from a selection among the more concrete elements offered it by the rich stream of life, a defensive shell of "fixed ideas." It is useless to speak kindly to the limpet. You must detach it by main force. That old comfortable clinging life, protected by its hard shell from the living waters of the sea, must now come to an end. A conflict of some kind—a severance of old habits, old notions, old prejudices—is here inevitable for you; and a decision as to the form which the new adjustments must take.

Now although in a general way we may regard the practical man's attitude to existence as a limpet-like adherence to the unreal, yet, from another point of view, fixity of purpose and desire is the last thing we can attribute to him. His mind is full of little whirlpools, twists and currents, conflicting systems, incompatible desires. One after another, he centers himself on ambition, love, duty, friendship, social convention, politics, religion, self-interest in one of its myriad forms, making of each a core round which whole sections of his life are arranged. One after another, these things either fail him or enslave him. Sometimes they become obsessions, distorting his judgment, narrowing his outlook, coloring his whole existence. Sometimes they develop inconsistent characters which involve him in public difficulties, private compromises, and self-deceptions of every kind. They split his attention, fritter his powers. This state of affairs, which usually passes for an "active life," begins to take on a different complexion when looked at with the simple eye of meditation. Then we observe that the plain man's world is in a muddle, just because he has tried to arrange its major interests round himself as round a center; and he is neither strong enough nor clever enough for the job. He has made a wretched little whirlpool in the mighty River of Becoming, interrupting—as he imagines, in his own interest—its even flow: and within that whirlpool are numerous petty complexes and countercurrents, among which his will and attention fly to and fro in a continual state of unrest. The man who makes a success of his life, in any department, is he who has chosen one from among these claims and interests, and devoted to it his energetic powers of heart and will, "unifying" himself about it, and from within it resisting all counterclaims. He has one objective, one center; has killed out the lesser ones, and simplified himself.

Now the artist, the discoverer, the philosopher, the lover, the patriot—the true enthusiast for any form of life—can only achieve the full reality to which his special art or passion gives access by innumerable renunciations. He must kill out the smaller centers of interest, in order that his whole will, love, and attention may pour itself out toward, seize upon, unite with, that special manifestation of the beauty and significance of the universe to which he is drawn. So, too, a deliberate self-simplification, a "purgation" of the heart and will, is demanded of those who would develop the form of consciousness called "mystical." All your power, all your resolution, is needed if you are to succeed in this adventure: there must be no frittering of energy, no mixture of motives. We hear much of the mystical temperament, the mystical vision. The mystical character is far more important: and its chief ingredients are courage, singleness of heart, and self-control. It is toward the perfecting of these military virtues, not to the production of a pious softness, that the discipline of asceticism is largely directed; and the ascetic foundation, in one form or another, is the only enduring foundation of a sane contemplative life.

You cannot, until you have steadied yourself, found a poise, and begun to resist some among the innumerable claims which the world of appearance perpetually makes upon your attention and your desire, make much use of the new power which Recollection has disclosed to you; and this Recollection itself, so long as it remains merely a matter of attention and does not involve the heart, is no better than a psychic trick. You are committed, therefore, as the fruit of your first attempts at self-knowledge, to a deliberate—probably a difficult—rearrangement of your character; to the stern course of self-discipline, the voluntary acts of choice on the one hand and of rejection on the other, which ascetic writers describe under the formidable names of Detachment and Mortification. By Detachment they mean the eviction of the limpet from its crevice; the refusal to anchor yourself to material things, to regard existence from the personal standpoint, or confuse custom with necessity. By Mortification they mean the resolving of the turbulent whirlpools and currents of your own conflicting passions, interests, desires; the killing out of all those tendencies which the peaceful vision of Recollection would condemn, and which create the fundamental opposition between your interior and exterior life.

What then, in the last resort, is the source of this opposition, the true reason of your uneasiness, your unrest? The reason lies, not in any real incompatibility between the interests of the temporal and the eternal orders, which are but two aspects of one Fact, two expressions of one Love. It lies solely in yourself; in your attitude toward the world of things. You are enslaved by the verb "to have": all your reactions to life consist in corporate or individual demands, appetites, wants. That "love of life" of which we sometimes speak is mostly cupboard-love. We are quick to snap at her ankles when she locks the larder door: a proceeding which we dignify by the name of "pessimism." The mystic knows not this attitude of demand. He tells us again and again that "he is rid of all his asking"; that "henceforth the heat of having shall never scorch him more." Compare this with your normal attitude to the world, practical man: your quiet certitude that you are well within your rights in pushing the claims of "the I, the Me, the Mine"; your habit, if you be religious, of asking for the weather and the government that you want, of persuading the Supernal Powers to take a special interest in your national or personal health and prosperity. How often in each day do you deliberately revert to an attitude of disinterested adoration? Yet this is the only attitude in which true communion with the universe is possible. The very mainspring of your activity is a demand, either for a continued possession of that which you have, or for something which as yet you have not: wealth, honor, success, social position, love, friendship, comfort, amusement. You feel that you have a right to some of these things: to a certain recognition of your powers, a certain immunity from failure or humiliation. You resent anything which opposes you in these matters. You become restless when you see other selves more skillful in the game of acquisition than yourself. You hold tight against all comers your own share of the spoils. You are rather inclined to shirk boring responsibilities and unattractive, unremunerative toil; are greedy of pleasure and excitement, devoted to the art of having a good time. If you possess a social sense, you demand these things not only for yourself but for your tribe—the domestic or racial group to which you belong. These dispositions, so ordinary that they almost pass unnoticed, were named by our blunt forefathers the Seven Deadly Sins of Pride, Anger, Envy, Avarice, Sloth, Gluttony, and Lust. Perhaps you would rather call them—as indeed they are—the seven common forms of egotism. They represent the natural reactions to life of the self-centered human consciousness, enslaved by the "world of multiplicity," and constitute absolute barriers to its attainment of Reality. So long as these dispositions govern character we can never see or feel things as they are; but only as they affect ourselves, our family, our party, our business, our church, our empire—the I, the Me, the Mine, in its narrower or wider manifestations. Only the detached and purified heart can view all things— the irrational cruelty of circumstance, the tortures of war, the apparent injustice of life, the acts and beliefs of enemy and friend—in true proportion, and reckon with calm mind the sum of evil and good. Therefore the mystics tell us perpetually that "selfhood must be killed" before Reality can be attained.

"Feel sin a lump, thou wottest never what, but none other thing than *thyself*," says *The Cloud of Unknowing*. "When the I, the Me, and the Mine are dead, the work of the Lord is done," says Kabir.[11] The substance of that wrongness of act and relation which constitutes "sin" is the separation of the individual spirit from the whole; the ridiculous megalomania which makes each man the center of his universe. Hence comes the turning inward and condensation of his energies and desires, till they do indeed form a "lump," a hard, tight core about which all the currents of his existence swirl. This

---

11. Kabir (1440–1518), an Indian sage of mixed Hindu and Muslim background. (Eds.)

heavy weight within the heart resists every outgoing impulse of the spirit, and tends to draw all things inward and downward to itself, never to pour itself forth in love, enthusiasm, sacrifice. "So long," says the *Theologia Germanica*,[12] "as a man seeketh his own will and his own highest good, because it is his, and for his own sake, he will never find it: for so long as he doeth this, he is not seeking his own highest good, and how then should he find it? For so long as he doeth this, he seeketh himself, and dreameth that he is himself the highest good. . . . But whosoever seeketh, loveth, and pursueth goodness, as goodness and for the sake of goodness, and maketh that his end—for nothing but the love of goodness, not for love of the I, Me, Mine, Self, and the like—he will find the highest good, for he seeketh it aright, and they who seek it otherwise do err."

So it is disinterestedness, the saint's and poet's love of things for their own sakes, the vision of the charitable heart, which is the secret of union with Reality and the condition of all real knowledge. This brings with it the precious quality of suppleness, the power of responding with ease and simplicity to the great rhythms of life; and this will only come when the ungainly "lump" of sin is broken, and the verb "to have," which expresses its reaction to existence, is ejected from the center of your con-

---

12. A work discovered and published by Martin Luther in 1516. (Eds.)

sciousness. Then your attitude to life will cease to be commercial, and become artistic. Then the guardian at the gate, scrutinizing and sorting the incoming impressions, will no longer ask, "What use is this to *me*?" before admitting the angel of beauty or significance who demands your hospitality. Then things will cease to have power over you. You will become free. "Son," says à Kempis,[13] "thou oughtest diligently to attend to this; that in every place, every action or outward occupation, thou be inwardly free and mighty in thyself, and all things be under thee, and thou not under them; that thou be lord and governor of thy deeds, not servant."

It is therefore by the withdrawal of your will from its feverish attachment to things, till "they are under thee and thou not under them," that you will gradually resolve the opposition between the recollective and the active sides of your personality. By diligent self-discipline, that mental attitude which the mystics sometimes call poverty and sometimes perfect freedom—for these are two aspects of one thing—will become possible to you. Ascending the mountain of self-knowledge and throwing aside your superfluous luggage as you go, you shall at last arrive at the point which they call the summit of the spirit, where the various forces of your character— brute energy, keen intellect, desirous heart—long

---

13. Thomas à Kempis (1380–1471), Augustinian monk and author of *The Imitation of Christ*. (Eds.)

dissipated among a thousand little wants and preferences, are gathered into one, and become a strong
and disciplined instrument wherewith your true self
can force a path deeper and deeper into the heart of
Reality.

Chapter VI
LOVE AND WILL

This steady effort toward the simplifying of your tangled character, its gradual emancipation from the fetters of the unreal, is not to dispense you from that other special training of the attention which the diligent practice of meditation and recollection effects. Your pursuit of the one must never involve neglect of the other; for these are the two sides—one moral, the other mental—of that unique process of self-conquest which Ruysbroeck calls "the gathering of the forces of the soul into the unity of the spirit": the welding together of all your powers, the focusing of them upon one point. Hence they should never, either in theory or practice, be separated. Only the act of recollection, the constantly renewed retreat to the quiet center of the spirit, gives that assurance of a Reality, a calmer and more valid life attainable by us, which supports the stress and pain of self-simplification and permits us to hope on, even in the teeth of the world's cruelty, indifference, degeneracy; while diligent character-building alone, with its perpetual untiring efforts at self-adjustment, its bracing, purging discipline, checks the human tendency to relapse into and react to the obvious, and makes possible the further development of the contemplative power.

So it is through and by these two great changes in your attitude toward things—first, the change of attention, which enables you to perceive a truer universe; next, the deliberate rearrangement of your ideas, energies, and desires in harmony with that which you have seen—that a progressive uniformity of life and experience is secured to you, and you are defended against the dangers of an indolent and useless mysticality. Only the real, say the mystics, can know Reality, for "we behold that which we are," the universe which we see is conditioned by the character of the mind that sees it: and this realness—since that which you seek is no mere glimpse of Eternal Life, but complete possession of it—must apply to every aspect of your being, the rich totality of character, all the "forces of the soul," not to some thin and isolated "spiritual sense" alone. This is why recollection and self-simplification—perception of, and adaptation to, the Spiritual World in which we dwell—are the essential preparations for the mystical life, and neither can exist in a wholesome and well-balanced form without the other. By them the mind, the will, the heart, which so long had dissipated their energies over a thousand scattered notions, wants, and loves, are gradually detached from their old exclusive preoccupation with the ephemeral interests of the self, or of the group to which the self belongs.

You, if you practice them, will find after a time—perhaps a long time—that the hard work which they involve has indeed brought about a profound and definite change in you. A new suppleness has taken the place of that rigidity which you have been accustomed to mistake for strength of character: an easier attitude toward the accidents of life. Your whole scale of values has undergone a silent transformation, since you have ceased to fight for your own hand and regard the nearest-at-hand world as the only one that counts. You have become, as the mystics would say, "free from inordinate attachments," the "heat of having" does not scorch you anymore; and because of this you possess great inward liberty, a sense of spaciousness and peace. Released from the obsessions which so long had governed them, will, heart, and mind are now all bent to the purposes of your deepest being: "gathered in the unity of the spirit," they have fused to become an agent with which it can act.

What form, then, shall this action take? It shall take a practical form, shall express itself in terms of movement: the pressing outward of the whole personality, the eager and trustful stretching of it toward the fresh universe which awaits you. As all scattered thinking was cut off in recollection, as all vagrant and unworthy desires have been killed by the exercises of detachment, so now all scattered willing, all hesitations between the indrawing and outflowing instincts of the soul, shall be checked and resolved. You are to *push* with all your power: not to absorb ideas, but to pour forth will and love. With this "conative act," as the psychologists would call it, the true contemplative life begins. Contemplation, you see, has no very close connection with dreaminess and idle musing: it is more like the intense effort of vision, the passionate and self-forgetful act of communion, presupposed in all creative art. It is, says one old English mystic, "a blind intent stretching . . . a privy love pressed" in the direction of Ultimate Beauty, athwart all the checks, hindrances, and contradictions of the restless world: a "loving stretching out" toward Reality, says the great Ruysbroeck,[14] than whom none has gone further on this path. Tension, ardor, are of its essence: it demands the perpetual exercise of industry and courage.

We observe in such definitions as these a strange neglect of that glory of man, the Pure Intellect, with which the spiritual prig enjoys to believe that he can climb up to the Empyrean itself. It almost seems as though the mystics shared Keats's view of the supremacy of feeling over thought, and reached out toward some new and higher range of sensation, rather than toward new and more accurate ideas. They are ever eager to assure us that man's most sublime thoughts of the Transcendent are but a little better than his worst: that loving intuition is the only certain guide. "By love may He be gotten and holden, but by thought never."

Yet here you are not to fall into the clumsy error of supposing that the things which are beyond the grasp of reason are necessarily unreasonable things. Immediate feeling, so far as it is true, does not oppose but transcends and completes the highest results of

---

14. Jan Van Ruysbroeck (1293–1381), Flemish mystic. (Eds.)

thought. It contains within itself the sum of all the processes through which thought would pass in the act of attaining the same goal: supposing thought to have reached—as it has not—the high pitch at which it was capable of thinking its way all along this road.

In the preliminary act of gathering yourself together, and in those unremitting explorations through which you came to "a knowing and a feeling of yourself as you are," thought assuredly had its place. There the powers of analysis, criticism, and deduction found work that they could do. But now it is the love and will—the feeling, the intent, the passionate desire—of the self which shall govern your activities and make possible your success. Few would care to brave the horrors of a courtship conducted upon strictly intellectual lines: and contemplation is an act of love, the wooing, not the critical study, of Divine Reality. It is an eager outpouring of ourselves toward a Somewhat Other for which we feel a passion of desire; a seeking, touching, and tasting, not a considering and analyzing, of the beautiful and true wherever found. It is, as it were, a responsive act of the organism to those Supernal Powers without, which touch and stir it. Deep humility as toward those Powers, a willing surrender to their control, is the first condition of success. The mystics speak much of these elusive contacts, felt more and more in the soul, as it becomes increasingly sensitive to the subtle movements of its spiritual environment.

Sense, feeling, taste, complacency, and sight,
These are the true and real joys,
The living, flowing, inward, melting, bright
And heavenly pleasures; all the rest are toys;
All which are founded in Desire
As light in flame and heat in fire.

But this new method of correspondence with the universe is not to be identified with "mere feeling" in its lowest and least orderly forms. Contemplation does not mean abject surrender to every "mystical" impression that comes in. It is no sentimental aestheticism or emotional piety to which you are being invited: nor shall the transcending of reason ever be achieved by way of spiritual silliness. All the powers of the self, raised to their intensest form, shall be used in it, though used perhaps in a new way. These, the three great faculties of love, thought, and will—with which you have been accustomed to make great show on the periphery of consciousness—you have, as it were, drawn inward during the course of your inward retreat: and by your education in detachment have cured them of their tendency to fritter their powers among a multiplicity of objects. Now, at the very heart of personality, you are alone with them; you hold with you in that "Interior Castle," and undistracted for the moment by the demands of practical existence, the three great tools wherewith the soul deals with life.

As regards the life you have hitherto looked upon as "normal," love—understood in its widest sense, as desire, emotional inclination—has throughout directed your activities. You did things, sought things, learned things, even suffered things, because at bottom you wanted to. Will has done the work to which love spurred it: thought has assimilated the results of their activities and made for them pictures, analyses, "explanations" of the world with which they had to deal. But now your purified love discerns and desires, your will is set toward, something which thought cannot really assimilate—still less explain. "Contemplation," says Ruysbroeck, "is a knowing that is in no wise ... therein all the workings of the reason fail." That reason has been trained to deal with the stuff of temporal existence. It will only make mincemeat of your experience of Eternity if you give it a chance; trimming, transforming, rationalizing that ineffable vision, trying to force it into a symbolic system with which the intellect can cope. This is why the great contemplatives utter again and again their solemn warning against the deceptiveness of thought when it ventures to deal with the spiritual intuitions of man, crying with the author of *The Cloud of Unknowing,* "Look that *nothing* live in thy working mind but a naked intent stretching"—the voluntary tension of your ever-growing, ever-moving personality pushing out toward the Real. "Love, and *do* what you like," said the wise Augustine: so little does mere surface activity count, against the deep motive that begets it.

The dynamic power of love and will, the fact that the heart's desire—if it be intense and industrious—is a better earnest of possible fulfillment than the most elegant theories of the spiritual world; this is the perpetual theme of all the Christian mystics. By such love, they think, the worlds themselves were made. By an eager outstretching toward Reality, they tell us, we tend to move toward Reality, to enter into its rhythm: by a humble and unquestioning surrender to it we permit its entrance into our souls. This twofold act, in which we find the double character of all true love—which both gives and takes, yields and demands—is assured, if we be patient and single-hearted, of ultimate success. At last our ignorance shall be done away; and we shall "apprehend" the real and the eternal, as we apprehend the sunshine when the sky is free from cloud. Therefore "Smite upon that thick cloud of unknowing with a sharp dart of longing love"—and suddenly it shall part, and disclose the blue.

"Smite," "press," "push," "strive"—these are strong words: yet they are constantly upon the lips of the contemplatives when describing the earlier stages of their art. Clearly, the abolition of discursive thought is not to absolve you from the obligations of industry. You are to "energize enthusiastically" upon new planes, where you shall see more intensely, hear more intensely, touch and taste more intensely than ever before: for the modes of communion which these senses make possible to you are now to operate as parts of the one single state of perfect intuition, of loving knowledge by union, to which you are growing up. And gradually you come to see that, if this be so, it is the ardent will that shall be the prime agent of your undertaking: a will which has now become the active expression of your deepest and purest desires. About this the recollected and simplified self is to gather itself as a center; and then to look out—steadily, deliberately—with eyes of love toward the world.

To "look with the eyes of love" seems a vague and sentimental recommendation: yet the whole art of spiritual communion is summed in it, and exact and important results flow from this exercise. The attitude which it involves is an attitude of complete humility and of receptiveness, without criticism, without clever analysis of the thing seen. When you look thus, you surrender your I-hood, see things at last as the artist does, for their sake, not for your own. The fundamental unity that is in you reaches out to the unity that is in them: and you achieve the "Simple Vision" of the poet and the mystic—that synthetic and undistorted apprehension of things which is the antithesis of the single vision of practical men. The doors of perception are cleansed, and everything appears as it is. The disfiguring results of hate, rivalry, prejudice, vanish away. Into that silent place to which recollection has brought you, new music, new color, new light are poured from the outward world.

The conscious love which achieves this vision may, indeed must, fluctuate—"As long as thou livest thou art subject to mutability; yea, though thou wilt not!" But the *will* which that love has enkindled can hold attention in the right direction. It can refuse to relapse to unreal and egotistic correspondences and continue, even in darkness, and in the suffering which such darkness brings to the awakened spirit, its appointed task, cutting a way into new levels of Reality.

Therefore this traditional stage in the development of the contemplative powers—in one sense the completion of their elementary schooling, in another the beginning of their true activities—is concerned with the toughening and further training of that will which self-simplification has detached from its old concentration upon the unreal wants and interests of the self. Merged with your intuitive love, this is to become the true agent of your encounter with Reality; for that Simple Eye of Intention, which is so supremely your own, and in the last resort the maker of your universe and controller of your destiny, is nothing else but a synthesis of such energetic will and such uncorrupt desire, turned and held in the direction of the Best.

Chapter VII

THE FIRST FORM OF
CONTEMPLATION

Concentration, recollection, a profound self-criticism, the stilling of his busy surface-intellect, his restless emotions of enmity and desire, the voluntary achievement of an attitude of disinterested love—by these strange paths the practical man has now been led, in order that he may know by communion something of the greater Life in which he is immersed and which he has so long and so successfully ignored. He has managed in his own small way something equivalent to those drastic purifications, those searching readjustments, which are undertaken by the heroic seekers for Reality; the arts whereby they defeat the tyranny of "the I, the Me, the Mine" and achieve the freedom of a wider life. Now, perhaps, he may share to some extent in that illumination, that extended and intensified perception of things, which they declare to be the heritage of the liberated consciousness.

This illumination shall be gradual. The attainment of it depends not so much upon a philosophy accepted, or a new gift of vision suddenly received, as upon an uninterrupted changing and widening of character; a progressive growth toward the Real, an ever more profound harmonization of the self's life with the greater and inclusive rhythms of existence. It shall therefore develop in width and depth as the sphere of that self's intuitive love extends. As your own practical sympathy with and understanding of other lives, your realization of them, may be narrowed and stiffened to include no more than the family group, or spread over your fellow workers, your class, your city, party, country, or religion— even perhaps the whole race—till you feel yourself utterly part of it, moving with it, suffering with it, and partake of its whole conscious life, so here. Self-mergence is a gradual process, dependent on a progressive unlimiting of personality. The apprehension of Reality which rewards it is gradual too. In essence, it is one continuous out-flowing movement toward that boundless heavenly consciousness where the "flaming ramparts" which shut you from true communion with all other selves and things is done away; an unbroken process of expansion and simplification, which is nothing more or less than the growth of the spirit of love, the full flowering of the patriotic sense. By this perpetually renewed casting down of the hard barriers of individuality, these willing submissions to the compelling rhythm of a larger existence than that of the solitary individual or even of the human group—by this perpetual widening, deepening, and unselfing of your attentiveness—you are to enlarge your boundaries and become the citizen of a greater, more joyous, more poignant world, the partaker of a more abundant life. The limits of this enlargement have not yet been discovered. The greatest contemplatives, returning from their highest ascents, can only tell us of a world that is "unwalled."

But this growth into higher realities, this blossoming of your contemplative consciousness—though it be, like all else we know in life, an unbroken process of movement and change—must be broken up and reduced to the series of concrete forms which we call "order" if our inelastic minds are to grasp it. So, we will consider it as the successive achievement of those three levels or manifestations of Reality, which we have agreed to call the Natural World of Becoming, the Metaphysical World of Being, and—last and highest—that Divine Reality within which these opposites are found as one. Though these three worlds of experience are so plaited together that intimations from the deeper layers of being constantly reach you through the natural scene, it is in this order of realization that you may best think of them, and of your own gradual upgrowth to the full stature of humanity. To elude nature, to refuse her friendship, and attempt to leap the river of life in the hope of finding God on the other side, is the common error of a perverted mysticality. It is as fatal in result as the opposite error of deliberately arrested development, which, being attuned to the wonderful rhythms of natural life, is content with this increase of sensibility, and, becoming a "nature mystic," asks no more.

So you are to begin with that first form of contemplation which the old mystics sometimes called the "discovery of God in His creatures." Not with some ecstatic adventure in supersensuous regions, but with the loving and patient exploration of the world that lies at your gates; the "ebb and flow and ever-during power" of which your own existence forms a part. You are to push back the self's barriers bit by bit, till at last all duration is included in the widening circles of its intuitive love: till you find in every manifestation of life—even those which you have petulantly classified as cruel or obscene—the ardent self-expression of that Immanent Being whose spark burns deep in your own soul.

The Indian mystics speak perpetually of the visible universe as the *Līlā* or Sport of God: the Infinite deliberately expressing Himself in finite form, the musical manifestation of His creative joy. All gracious and all courteous souls, they think, will gladly join His play, considering rather the wonder and achievement of the whole—its vivid movement, its strange and terrible evocations of beauty from torment, nobility from conflict and death, its mingled splendor of sacrifice and triumph—than their personal conquests, disappointments, and fatigues. In the first form of contemplation you are to realize the movement of this game, in which you have played so long a languid and involuntary part, and find your own place in it. It is flowing, growing, changing, making perpetual unexpected patterns within the evolving melody of the Divine Thought. In all things it is incomplete, unstable; and so are you. Your fellow men, enduring on the battlefield, living and breeding in the slum, adventurous and studious, sensuous and pure—more, your great comrades, the hills, the trees, the rivers, the darting birds, the scuttering insects, the little soft populations of the grass—all these are playing with you. They move one to another in delicate responsive measures, now violent, now gentle, now in conflict, now in peace, yet ever weaving the pattern of a ritual dance, and obedient to the music of that invisible Choragus whom Boehme and Plotinus[15] knew. What is that great wind which blows without, in continuous and ineffable harmonies? Part of you, practical man. There is but one music in the world: and to it you contribute perpetually, whether you will or no, your one little ditty of no tone.

Mad with joy, life and death dance to the rhythm of this
music:
The hills and the sea and the earth dance:
The world of man dances in laughter and tears.[16]

It seems a pity to remain in ignorance of this, to keep as it were a plate-glass window between yourself and your fellow dancers—all those other thoughts of God, perpetually becoming, changing, and growing beside you—and commit yourself to the unsocial attitude of the "cat that walks by itself."

---

15. Jacob Boehme (1575–1624), German mystic and author of *The Way to Christ* (1624). Plotinus (205–270 C.E.), Egyptian philosopher and founder of Neoplatonism. (Eds.)

16. From the poems of Kabir, see note, p. 59. (Eds.)

Begin therefore at once. Gather yourself up, as the exercises of recollection have taught you to do. Then—with attention no longer frittered among the petty accidents and interests of your personal life, but poised, tense, ready for the work you shall demand of it—stretch out by a distinct act of loving will toward one of the myriad manifestations of life that surround you: and which, in an ordinary way, you hardly notice unless you happen to need them. Pour yourself out toward it, do not draw its image toward you. Deliberate—more, impassioned—attentiveness, an attentiveness which soon transcends all consciousness of yourself, as separate from and attending to the thing seen: this is the condition of success. As to the object of contemplation, it matters little. From Alp to insect, anything will do, provided that your attitude be right: for all things in this world toward which you are stretching out are linked together, and one truly apprehended will be the gateway to the rest.

Look with the eye of contemplation on the most dissipated tabby of the streets, and you shall discern the celestial quality of life set like an aureole about his tattered ears, and hear in his strident mew an echo of

> *The deep enthusiastic joy,*
> *The rapture of the hallelujah sent*
> *From all that breathes and is.*[17]

----

17. From William Wordsworth (1770–1850), *The Prelude,* Book Fourteenth, ll. 293–95. (Eds.)

The sooty tree up which he scrambles to escape your earnest gaze is holy too. It contains for you the whole divine cycle of the seasons; upon the plane of quiet, its inward pulse is clearly to be heard. But you must look at these things as you would look into the eyes of a friend: ardently, selflessly, without considering his reputation, his practical uses, his anatomical peculiarities, or the vices which might emerge were he subjected to psychoanalysis.

Such a simple exercise, if entered upon with singleness of heart, will soon repay you. By this quiet yet tense act of communion, this loving gaze, you will presently discover a relationship—far more intimate than anything you imagined—between yourself and the surrounding "objects of sense"; and in those objects of sense a profound significance, a personal quality, and actual power of response, which you might in cooler moments think absurd. Making good your correspondences with these fellow travelers, you will learn to say with Whitman:

You air that serves me with breath to speak!
You objects that call from diffusion my meanings and
give them shape!
You light that wraps me and all things in delicate
equable showers!
You paths worn in the irregular hollows by the roadside!
I believe you are latent with unseen existences, you are
so dear to me.[18]

---

18. From Walt Whitman (1819–92), "Song of the Open Road." (Eds.)

A subtle interpenetration of your spirit with the spirit of those "unseen existences," now so deeply and thrillingly felt by you, will take place. Old barriers will vanish: and you will become aware that St. Francis was accurate as well as charming when he spoke of Brother Wind and Sister Water, and that Stevenson was obviously right when he said that since

> *The world is so full of a number of things,*
> *I'm sure we ought all to be happy as kings.*[19]

Those glad and vivid "things" will speak to you. They will offer you news at least as definite and credible as that which the paperboy is hawking in the street: direct messages from that Beauty which the artist reports at best at second hand. Because of your new sensitiveness, anthems will be heard of you from every gutter; poems of intolerable loveliness will bud for you on every weed. Best and greatest, your fellowmen will shine for you with new significance and light. Humility and awe will be evoked in you by the beautiful and patient figures of the poor, their long dumb heroisms, their willing acceptance of the burden of life. All the various members of the human group, the little children and the aged, those who stand for energy, those dedicated to skill, to thought, to plainest service, or to prayer, will have

---

19. Robert Louis Stevenson (1850–94), "Happy Thought." (Eds.)

for you fresh vivid significance, be felt as part of your own wider being. All adventurous endeavors, all splendor of pain and all beauty of play—more, that gray unceasing effort of existence which makes up the groundwork of the social web, and the ineffective hopes, enthusiasms, and loves which transfuse it—all these will be seen and felt by you at last as full of glory, full of meaning; for you will see them with innocent, attentive, disinterested eyes, feel them as infinitely significant and adorable parts of the Transcendent Whole in which you also are immersed.

This discovery of your fraternal link with all living things, this down-sinking of your arrogant personality into the great generous stream of life, marks an important stage in your apprehension of that Science of Love which contemplation is to teach. You are not to confuse it with pretty fancies about nature, such as all imaginative persons enjoy; still less, with a self-conscious and deliberate humanitarianism. It is a veritable condition of awareness; a direct perception, not an opinion or an idea. For those who attain it, the span of the senses is extended. These live in a world which is lit with an intenser light; has, as George Fox[20] insisted, "another smell than before." They hear all about them the delicate music of growth, and see the "new color" of which the mystics speak.

---

20. George Fox (1624–91), founder in England of the Society of Friends. (Eds.)

Further, you will observe that this act, and the attitude which is proper to it, differs in a very important way even from that special attentiveness which characterized the stage of meditation, and which seems at first sight to resemble it in many respects. Then, it was an idea or image from among the common stock—one of those conceptual labels with which the human paste brush has decorated the surface of the universe—which you were encouraged to hold before your mind. Now, turning away from the label, you shall surrender yourself to the direct message poured out toward you by the *thing*. Then, you considered: now, you are to absorb. This experience will be, in the very highest sense, the experience of sensation without thought: the essential sensation, the "savoring" to which some of the mystics invite us, of which our fragmentary bodily senses offer us a transient sacrament. So here at last, in this intimate communion, this "simple seeing," this total surrender of you to the impress of things, you are using to the full the sacred powers of sense: and so using them, because you are concentrating upon them, accepting their reports in simplicity. You have, in this contemplative outlook, carried the peculiar methods of artistic apprehension to their highest stage: with the result that the sense-world has become for you, as Erigena[21] said that all creatures were, "a theophany, or appearance of God." Not, you observe, a

---

21. Johannes Scotus Erigena (c. 810–c. 877), Irish theologian and Neoplatonist. (Eds.)

symbol, but a showing: a very different thing. You have begun now the Plotinian ascent from multiplicity to unity, and therefore begin to perceive in the Many the clear and actual presence of the One: the changeless and absolute Life, manifesting itself in all the myriad nascent, crescent, cadent lives. Poets, gazing thus at the "flower in the crannied wall" or the "green thing that stands in the way," have been led deep into the heart of its life, there to discern the secret of the universe.

All the greater poems of Wordsworth and Walt Whitman represent an attempt to translate direct contemplative experience of this kind into words and rhythms which might convey its secret to other men: all Blake's philosophy is but a desperate effort to persuade us to exchange the false world of "Nature" on which we usually look—and which is not really Nature at all—for this, the true world, to which he gave the confusing name of "Imagination." For these, the contemplation of the World of Becoming assumes the intense form which we call genius: even to read their poems is to feel the beating of a heart, the upleap of a joy, greater than anything that we have known. Yet your own little efforts toward the attainment of this level of consciousness will at least give to you, together with a more vivid universe, a wholly new comprehension of their works and that of other poets and artists who have drunk from the chalice of the Spirit of Life. These works are now observed by you to be the only artistic creations to which the name of Realism is appropriate; and it is by the standard of reality that you shall now criticize them, recognizing in utterances which you once dismissed as rhetoric the desperate efforts of the clear-sighted toward the exact description of things veritably seen in that simplified state of consciousness which Blake called "imagination uncorrupt."

It was from those purified and heightened levels of perception to which the first form of contemplation inducts the soul that Julian of Norwich,[22] gazing upon "a little thing, the quantity of an hazelnut," found in it the epitome of all that was made; for therein she perceived the royal character of life. So small and helpless in its mightiest forms, so august even in its meanest, that life in its wholeness was then realized by her as the direct outbirth of, and the meek dependent upon, the Energy of Divine Love. She felt at once the fugitive character of its apparent existence, the perdurable Reality within which it was held. "I marveled," she said, "how it might last, for methought it might suddenly have fallen to naught for littleness. And I was answered in my understanding: *It lasteth, and ever shall, for that God loveth it.* And so All-thing hath the being by the love of God." To this same apprehension of Reality, this linking up of each finite expression with its Origin, this search for the inner significance of every fragment of life, one of the greatest and most balanced contemplatives of the nineteenth century, Florence

---

22. Dame Julian of Norwich (c. 1342–?), English anchoress and contemplative. Wrote *Revelations of Divine Love.* (Eds.)

Nightingale, reached out when she exclaimed in an hour of self-examination, "I must strive to see only God in my friends, and God in my cats."

Yet it is not the self-tormenting strife of introspective and self-conscious aspiration, but rather an unrelaxed, diligent intention, a steady acquiescence, a simple and loyal surrender to the great currents of life, a holding on to results achieved in your best moments, that shall do it for you: a surrender not limp but deliberate, a trustful self-donation, a "living faith." "A pleasing stirring of love," says *The Cloud of Unknowing;* not a desperate anxious struggle for more light. True contemplation can only thrive when defended from two opposite exaggerations: quietism on the one hand, and spiritual fuss upon the other. Neither from passivity nor from anxiety has it anything to gain. Though the way may be long, the material of your mind intractable, to the eager lover of Reality ultimate success is assured. The strong tide of Transcendent Life will inevitably invade, clarify, uplift the consciousness which is open to receive it, a movement from without—subtle yet actual—answering each willed movement from within. "Your opening and His entering," says Eckhart,[23] "are but one moment." When, therefore, you put aside your preconceived ideas, your self-centered scale of values, and let intuition have its way with you, you open up by this act new levels of the world. Such an

---

23. Meister Eckhart (1260–1328), German Dominican preacher and theologian. Accused and exonerated of heresy. (Eds.)

opening up is the most practical of all activities; for then and then only will your diurnal existence, and the natural scene in which that existence is set, begin to give up to you its richness and meaning. Its paradoxes and inequalities will be disclosed as true constituents of its beauty, an inconceivable splendor will be shaken out from its dingiest folds. Then, and only then, escaping the single vision of the selfish, you will begin to guess all that your senses were meant to be.

I swear the earth shall surely be complete to him or her
    who shall be complete.
The earth remains jagged and broken only to him or her
    who remains jagged and broken.[24]

---

24. From Whitman, "A Song of the Rolling Earth." (Eds.)

Chapter VIII
THE SECOND FORM OF CONTEMPLATION

"And here," says Ruysbroeck of the self which has reached this point, "there begins a hunger and a thirst which shall never more be stilled."

In the First Form of Contemplation that self has been striving to know better its own natural plane of existence. It has stretched out the feelers of its intuitive love into the general stream of duration of which it is a part. Breaking down the fences of personality, merging itself in a larger consciousness, it has learned to know the World of Becoming from within—as a citizen, a member of the great society of life, not merely as a spectator. But the more deeply and completely you become immersed in and aware of this life, the greater the extension of your consciousness; the more insistently will rumors and intimations of a higher plane of experience, a closer unity and more complete synthesis, begin to besiege you. You feel that hitherto you have received the messages of life in a series of disconnected words and notes, from which your mind constructed as best it could certain coherent sentences and tunes— laws, classifications, relations, and the rest. But now you reach out toward the ultimate sentence and melody, which exist independently of your own constructive efforts, and realize that the words and notes which so often puzzled you by displaying an intensity that exceeded the demands of your little world only have beauty and meaning just because and insofar as you discern them to be the partial expressions of a greater whole which is still beyond your reach.

You have long been like a child tearing up the petals of flowers in order to make a mosaic on the garden path; and the results of this murderous diligence you mistook for a knowledge of the world. When the bits fitted with unusual exactitude, you called it science. Now at last you have perceived the greater truth and loveliness of the living plant from which you broke them: have, in fact, entered into direct communion with it, "united" with its reality. But this very recognition of the living, growing plant does and must entail for you a consciousness of deeper realities, which, as yet, you have not touched: of the intangible things and forces which feed and support it; of the whole universe that touches you through its life. A mere cataloging of all the plants—though this were far better than your old game of indexing your own poor photographs of them—will never give you access to the Unity, the Fact, whatever it may be, which manifests itself through them. To suppose that it can do so is the cardinal error of the "nature mystic": an error parallel with that of the psychologist who looks for the soul in "psychic states."

The deeper your realization of the plant in its wonder, the more perfect your union with the world of growth and change, the quicker, the more subtle your response to its countless suggestions, so much the more acute will become your craving for Something More. You will now find and feel the Infinite and Eternal, making as it were veiled and sacramental contacts with you under these accidents—through these its ceaseless creative activities—and you will want to press through and beyond them, to a fuller realization of, a more perfect and unmediated union with, the Substance of all That Is. With the great widening and deepening of your life that has ensued from the abolition of a narrow selfhood, your entrance into the larger consciousness of living things, there has necessarily come to you an instinctive knowledge of a final and absolute group relation, transcending and including all lesser unions in its sweep. To this, the second stage of contemplation, in which human consciousness enters into its peculiar heritage, something within you now seems to urge you on.

If you obey this inward push, pressing forward with the "sharp dart of your longing love," forcing the point of your willful attention further and further into the web of things, such an ever-deepening realization, such an extension of your conscious life, will indeed become possible to you. Nothing but your own apathy, your feeble and limited desire, limits this realization. Here there is a strict relation between demand and supply—your achievement shall be in proportion to the greatness of your desire. The fact, and the in-pressing energy, of the Reality without does not vary. Only the extent to which you are able to receive it depends upon your courage and generosity, the measure in which you give yourself to its embrace. Those minds which set a limit to their self-donation must feel, as they attain it, not a sense of satisfaction but a sense of constriction. It is useless to offer your spirit a garden—even a garden inhabited by saints and angels—and pretend that it has been made free of the universe. You will not have peace until you do away with all banks and hedges, and exchange the garden for the wilderness that is unwalled, that wild strange place of silence where "lovers lose themselves."

Yet you must begin this great adventure humbly; and take, as Julian of Norwich did, the first stage of your new outward-going journey along the road that lies nearest at hand. When Julian looked with the eye of contemplation upon that "little thing" which revealed to her the oneness of the created universe, her deep and loving sight perceived in it successively three properties, which she expressed as well as she might under the symbols of her own theology: "The first is that God made it; the second is that God loveth it; the third is that God keepeth it." Here are three phases in the ever-widening contemplative apprehension of Reality. Not three opinions, but three facts, for which she struggles to find words. The first is that each separate living thing, budding "like an hazel nut" upon the tree of life, and there destined to mature, age, and die, is the outbirth of another power, of a creative push: that the World of Becoming in all its richness and variety is not ultimate, but formed by Something other than, and utterly transcendent to, itself. This, of course, the religious mind invariably takes for granted: but we are concerned with immediate experience rather than faith. To feel and know those two aspects of Reality which we call "created" and "uncreated," nature and spirit—to be as sharply aware of them, as sure of them, as we are of land and sea—is to be made free of the supersensual world. It is to stand for an instant at the Poet's side, and see that Poem of which you have deciphered separate phrases in the earlier form of contemplation. Then you were learning to read and found in the words, the lines, the stanzas an astonishing meaning and loveliness. But how much greater the significance of every detail would appear to you, how much more truly you would possess its life, were you acquainted with the Poem: not as a mere succession of such lines and stanzas, but as a nonsuccessional whole.

From this Julian passes to that deeper knowledge of the heart which comes from a humble and disinterested acceptance of life; that this Creation, this whole changeful natural order, with all its apparent collisions, cruelties, and waste, yet springs from an ardor, an immeasurable love, a perpetual donation, which generates it, upholds it, drives it; for "all-thing hath the being by the love of God." Blake's anguished question here receives its answer: the Mind that conceived the lamb conceived the tiger too. Everything, says Julian in effect, whether gracious, terrible, or malignant, is enwrapped in love and is part of a world produced not by mechanical necessity, but by passionate desire. Therefore nothing can really be mean, nothing despicable; nothing, however perverted, irredeemable. The blasphemous other-worldliness of the false mystic who conceives of matter as an evil thing and flies from its "deceits" is corrected by this loving sight. Hence, the more beautiful and noble a thing appears to us, the more we love it—so much the more truly do we see it: for then we perceive within it the Divine ardor surging up toward expression, and share that simplicity and purity of vision in which most saints and some poets see all things "as they are in God."

Lastly, this love-driven world of duration—this work within which the Divine Artist passionately and patiently expresses His infinite dream under finite forms—is held in another, mightier embrace. It is "kept," says Julian. Paradoxically, the perpetual changeful energies of love and creation which inspire it are gathered up and made complete within the unchanging fact of Being: the Eternal and Absolute, within which the world of things is set as the tree is set in the supporting earth, the enfolding air. There, finally, is the rock and refuge of the seeking consciousness wearied by the ceaseless process of the flux. There that flux exists in its wholeness, "all at once," in a manner which we can never comprehend, but which in hours of withdrawal we may sometimes taste and feel. It is in man's moments of contact with this, when he penetrates beyond all images, however lovely, however significant, to that ineffable awareness which the mystics call "Naked Contemplation"—since it is stripped of all the clothing with which reason and imagination drape and disguise both our devils and our gods—that the hunger and thirst of the heart is satisfied, and we receive indeed an assurance of ultimate Reality. This assurance is not the cool conclusion of a successful argument. It is rather the seizing at last of Something which we have ever felt near us and enticing us: the unspeakably simple because completely inclusive solution of all the puzzles of life.

As, then, you gave yourself to the broken-up yet actual reality of the natural world, in order that it might give itself to you, and your possession of its secret was achieved, first by surrender of selfhood, next by a diligent thrusting out of your attention, last by a union of love; so now by a repetition upon fresh levels of that same process, you are to mount up to higher unions still. Held tight as it seems to you in the finite, committed to the perpetual rhythmic changes, the unceasing flux of "natural" life— compelled to pass on from state to state, to grow, to age, to die—there is yet, as you discovered in the first exercise of recollection, something in you which endures through and therefore transcends this world of change. This inhabitant, this mobile spirit, can spread and merge in the general consciousness, and gather itself again to one intense point of personality. It has too an innate knowledge of—an instinct for—another, greater rhythm, another order of Reality, as yet outside its conscious field; or, as we say, a capacity for the Infinite. This capacity, this unfulfilled craving, which the cunning mind of the practical man suppresses and disguises as best it can, is the source of all your unrest. More, it is the true origin of all your best loves and enthusiasms, the inspiring cause of your heroisms and achievements, which are but oblique and tentative efforts to still that strange hunger for some final object of devotion, some completing and elucidating vision, some total self-donation, some great and perfect Act within which your little activity can be merged.

St. Thomas Aquinas says that a man is only withheld from this desired vision of the Divine Essence, this discovery of the Pure Act (which indeed is everywhere pressing in on him and supporting him), by the apparent necessity which he is under of turning to bodily images, of breaking up his continuous and living intuition into conceptual scraps; in other words, because he cannot live the life of sensation without thought. But it is not the man, it is merely his mental machinery which is under this "necessity." This it is which translates, analyzes, incorporates in finite images the boundless perceptions of the spirit, passing through its prism the White Light of Reality, and shattering it to a succession of colored rays. Therefore, the man who would know the Divine Secret must unshackle himself more thoroughly than ever before from the tyranny of the image-making power. As it is not by the methods of the laboratory that we learn to know life, so it is not by the methods of the intellect that we learn to know God.

"For of all other creatures and their works," says the author of *The Cloud of Unknowing,* "yea, and of the works of God's self, may a man through grace have full-head of knowing, and well he can think of them: but of God Himself can no man think. And therefore I would leave all that thing that I can think, and choose to my love that thing that I cannot think. For why; He may well be loved, but not thought. By love may He be gotten and holden; but by thought never."

"Gotten and holden": homely words that suggest rather the outstretching of the hand to take something lying at your very gates, than the long outward journey or terrific ascent of the contemplative soul. Reality indeed, the mystics say, is "near and far"; far from our thoughts, but saturating and supporting our lives. Nothing would be nearer, nothing dearer, nothing sweeter, were the doors of our perception truly cleansed. You have then but to focus attention upon your own deep reality, "realize your own soul," in order to find it. "We dwell in Him and He in us": you participate in the Eternal Order now. The vision of the Divine Essence—the participation of its own small activity in the Supernal Act—is for the spark of your soul a perpetual process. On the apex of your personality, spirit ever gazes upon Spirit, melts and merges in it: from and by this encounter its life arises and is sustained. But you have been busy from your childhood with other matters. All the urgent affairs of "life," as you absurdly called it, have monopolized your field of consciousness. Thus all the important events of your real life, physical and spiritual—the mysterious perpetual growth of you, the knitting up of fresh bits of the universe into the unstable body which you confuse with yourself, the hum and whirr of the machine which preserves your contacts with the material world, the more delicate movements which condition your correspondences with, and growth within, the spiritual order—all these have gone on unperceived by you. All the time you have been kept and nourished, like the "Little Thing," by an enfolding and creative love; yet of this you are less conscious than you are of the air that you breathe.

Now, as in the first stage of contemplation you learned and established, as a patent and experienced fact, your fraternal relation with all the other children of God, entering into the rhythm of their existence, participating in their stress and their joy, will you not at least try to make patent this your filial relation too? This actualization of your true status, your place in the Eternal World, is waiting for you. It represents the next phase in your gradual achievement of Reality. The method by which you will attain to it is strictly analogous to that by which you obtained a more vivid awareness of the natural world in which you grow and move. Here too it shall be direct, intuitive contact, sensation rather than thought, which shall bring you certitude— "tasting food, not talking about it," as St. Bonaventura says.

Yet there is a marked difference between these two stages. In the first, the deliberate inward retreat and gathering together of your faculties which was effected by recollection was the prelude to a new coming forth, an outflow from the narrow limits of a merely personal life to the better and truer apprehension of the created world. Now, in the second stage, the disciplined and recollected attention seems to take an opposite course. It is directed toward a plane of existence with which your bodily senses have no attachments: which is not merely misrepresented by your ordinary concepts, but cannot be represented by them at all. It must therefore sink inward toward its own center, "away from all that can be thought or felt," as the mystics say, "away from every image, every notion, every thing," toward that strange condition of obscurity which St. John of the Cross calls the "Night of Sense." Do this steadily, checking each vagrant instinct, each insistent thought, however "spiritual" it may seem, pressing ever more deeply inward toward that ground, that simple and undifferentiated Being from which your diverse faculties emerge. Presently you will find yourself, emptied and freed, in a place stripped bare of all the machinery of thought, and achieve the condition of simplicity which those same specialists call nakedness of spirit or "Wayless Love," and which they declare to be above all human images and ideas—a state of consciousness in which "all the workings of the reason fail." Then you will observe that you have entered into an intense and vivid silence: a silence which exists in itself, through and in spite of the ceaseless noises of your normal world. Within this world of silence you seem as it were to lose yourself, "to ebb and to flow, to wander and be lost in the Imageless Ground," says Ruysbroeck, struggling to describe the sensations of the self in this, its first initiation into the "wayless world, beyond image," where "all is, yet in no wise."

Yet in spite of the darkness that enfolds you, the Cloud of Unknowing into which you have plunged, you are sure that it is well to be here. A peculiar certitude which you cannot analyze, a strange satisfaction and peace, is distilled into you. You begin to understand what the Psalmist meant when he said, "Be still, and know."[25] You are lost in a wilderness, a solitude, a dim strange state of which you can say nothing, since it offers no material to your image-making mind. But this wilderness, from one point of view so bare and desolate, from another is yet strangely homely. In it, all your sorrowful questionings are answered without utterance; it is the All, and you are within it and part of it, and know that it is good. It calls forth the utmost adoration of which you are capable, and, mysteriously, gives love for love. You have ascended now, say the mystics, into the Freedom of the Will of God; are become part of a higher, slower duration, which carries you as it were upon its bosom and—though never perhaps before has your soul been so truly active—seems to you a stillness, a rest.

The doctrine of Plotinus concerning a higher life of unity, a lower life of multiplicity, possible to every human spirit, will now appear to you not a fantastic theory, but a plain statement of fact, which you have verified in your own experience. You perceive that these are the two complementary ways of appre-

---

25. "Be still, and know that I am God," King James Version, Psalm 46:10. (Eds.)

hending and uniting with Reality—the one as a dynamic process, the other as an eternal whole. Thus understood, they do not conflict. You know that the flow, the broken-up world of change and multiplicity, is still going on; and that you, as a creature of the time-world, are moving and growing with it. But, thanks to the development of the higher side of your consciousness, you are now lifted to a new poise, a direct participation in that simple, transcendent life "broken, yet not divided," which gives to this time-world all its meaning and validity. And you know, without derogation from the realness of that life of flux within which you first made good your attachments to the universe, that you are also a true constituent of the greater whole, that since you are man, you are also spirit, and are living Eternal Life now, in the midst of time.

The effect of this form of contemplation, in the degree in which the ordinary man may learn to practice it, is like the sudden change of atmosphere, the shifting of values, which we experience when we pass from the busy streets into a quiet church, where a lamp burns, and a silence reigns, the same yesterday, today, and forever. Thence is poured forth a stillness which strikes through the tumult without. Eluding the flicker of the arc lamps, thence through an upper window we may glimpse a perpetual star.

The walls of the church, limiting the range of our attention, shutting out the torrent of life, with its insistent demands and appeals, make possible our apprehension of this deep eternal peace. The character of our consciousness, intermediate between Eternity and Time, and ever ready to swing between them, makes such a device, such a concrete aid to concentration, essential to us. But the peace, the presence, is everywhere—for us, not for it, is the altar and the sanctuary required—and your deliberate, humble practice of contemplation will teach you at last to find it, outside the sheltering walls of recollection as well as within. You will realize then what Julian meant when she declared the ultimate property of all that was made to be that "God keepeth it": will *feel* the violent consciousness of an enfolding Presence, utterly transcending the fluid, changeful nature-life, and incomprehensible to the intelligence which that nature-life has developed and trained. And as you knew the secret of that nature-life best by surrendering yourself to it, by entering its currents, and refusing to analyze or arrange: so here, by a deliberate giving of yourself to the silence, the rich "nothingness," the "Cloud," you will draw nearest to the Reality it conceals from the eye of sense. "Lovers put out the candle and draw the curtains," says Patmore, "when they wish to see the God and the Goddess: and in the higher communion, the night of thought is the light of perception."[26]

Such an experience of Eternity, the attainment of that intuitive awareness, that meek and simple self-mergence, which the mystics call sometimes, according to its degree and special circumstances,

---

26. From Coventry Patmore (1823–96), English poet and writer, *The Angel in the House,* a collection of poems. (Eds.)

the Quiet, the Desert of God, the Divine Dark, represents the utmost that human consciousness can do of itself toward the achievement of union with Reality. To some it brings joy and peace, to others fear: to all a paradoxical sense of the lowliness and greatness of the soul, which now at last can measure itself by the august standards of the Infinite. Though the trained and diligent will of the contemplative can, if control of the attention be really established, recapture this state of awareness, retreat into the Quiet again and again, yet, it is of necessity a fleeting experience; for man is immersed in duration, subject to it. Its demands upon his attention can only cease with the cessation of physical life—perhaps not then. Perpetual absorption in the Transcendent is a human impossibility, and the effort to achieve it is both unsocial and silly. But this experience, this "ascent to the Nought," changes forever the proportions of the life that once has known it; gives to it depth and height, and prepares the way for those further experiences, that great transfiguration of existence which comes when the personal activity of the finite will gives place to the great and compelling action of another Power.

Chapter IX

THE THIRD FORM OF CONTEMPLATION

The hard separation which some mystical writers insist upon making between "natural" and "super-natural" contemplation has been on the whole pro-ductive of confusion rather than clearness: for the word "supernatural" has many unfortunate associa-tions for the mind of the plain man. It at once sug-gests to him visions and ecstasies, superstitious beliefs, ghosts, and other disagreeable interferences with the order which he calls "natural"; and inclines him to his old attitude of suspicion in respect of all mystical things. But some word we must have, to indicate the real cleavage which exists between the second and third stages in the development of the contemplative consciousness: the real change which, if you would go further on these interior paths, must now take place in the manner of your apprehension of Reality. Hitherto, all that you have attained has been—or at least has seemed to you—the direct result of your own hard work. A difficult self-discipline, the slowly achieved control of your vagrant thoughts and desires, the steady daily practice of recollection, a diligent pushing out of your consciousness from the superficial to the fundamental, an unselfish lov-ing attention: all this has been rewarded by the

gradual broadening and deepening of your perceptions, by an initiation into the movements of a larger
life. You have been a knocker, a seeker, an asker:
have beaten upon the Cloud of Unknowing "with
a sharp dart of longing love." A perpetual effort of
the will has characterized your inner development.
Your contemplation, in fact, as the specialists would
say, has been "active," not "infused."

But now, having achieved an awareness—obscure
and indescribable indeed, yet actual—of the enfolding presence of Reality, under those two forms which
the theologians call the "immanence" and the "transcendence" of the Divine, a change is to take place in
the relation between your finite human spirit and
the Infinite Life in which at last it knows itself to
dwell. All that will now come to you—and much
perhaps will come—will happen as it seems without
effort on your own part: though really it will be the
direct result of that long stress and discipline which
has gone before, and has made it possible for you to
feel the subtle contact of deeper realities. It will
depend also on the steady continuance—often perhaps through long periods of darkness and boredom—of that poise to which you have been trained:
the stretching out of the loving and surrendered will
into the dimness and silence, the continued trustful
habitation of the soul in the atmosphere of the
Essential World. You are like a traveler arrived in a
new country. The journey has been a long one; and
the hardships and obstacles involved in it, the effort,
the perpetual conscious pressing forward, have at
last come to seem the chief features of your inner

life. Now, with their cessation, you feel curiously lost, as if the chief object of your existence has been taken away. No need to push on any further: yet, though there is no more that you can do of yourself, there is much that may and must be done to you. The place that you have come to seems strange and bewildering, for it lies far beyond the horizons of human thought. There are no familiar landmarks, nothing on which you can lay hold. You "wander to and fro," as the mystics say, "in this fathomless ground," surrounded by silence and darkness, struggling to breathe this rarefied air. Like those who go to live in new latitudes, you must become acclimatized. Your state, then, should now be wisely passive; in order that the great influences which surround you may take and adjust your spirit, that the unaccustomed light, which now seems to you a darkness, may clarify your eyes, and that you may be transformed from a visitor into an inhabitant of that supernal Country which St. Augustine described as "no mere vision, but a home."

You are therefore to let yourself go; to cease all conscious, anxious striving and pushing. Finding yourself in this place of darkness and quietude, this "Night of the Spirit," as St. John of the Cross has called it, you are to dwell there meekly, asking nothing, seeking nothing, but with your doors flung wide open toward God. And as you do thus, there will come to you an ever-clearer certitude that this darkness enveils the goal for which you have been seeking from the first: the final Reality with which you are destined to unite, the perfect satisfaction of your most ardent and most sacred desires. It is there, but you cannot by your efforts reach it. This realization of your own complete impotence, of the resistance which the Transcendent—long sought and faithfully served—now seems to offer to your busy outgoing will and love, your ardor, your deliberate self-donation, is at once the most painful and most essential phase in the training of the human soul. It brings you into that state of passive suffering which is to complete the decentralization of your character, test the purity of your love, and perfect your education in humility.

Here, you must oppose more thoroughly than ever before the instincts and suggestions of your separate, clever, energetic self, which, hating silence and dimness, is always trying to take the methods of Martha into the domain of Mary, and seldom discriminates between passivity and sloth. Perhaps you will find, when you try to achieve this perfect self-abandonment, that a further, more drastic self-exploration, a deeper, more searching purification than that which was forced upon you by your first experience of the recollective state, is needed. The last fragments of selfhood, the very desire for spiritual satisfaction—the fundamental human tendency to drag down the Simple Fact and make it ours, instead of offering ourselves to it—must be sought out and killed. In this deep contemplation, this profound Quiet, your soul gradually becomes conscious of a constriction, a dreadful narrowness of personality: something still existing in itself, still tending to draw inward to its own center, and keeping it from that absolute surrender which is the only way to peace. An attitude of perfect generosity, complete submission, willing acquiescence in anything that may happen—even in failure and death—is here your only hope: for union with Reality can only be a union of love, a glad and humble self-mergence in the universal life. You must, so far as you are able, give yourself up to, "die into," melt into the Whole, abandon all efforts to lay hold of It. More, you must be willing that it should lay hold of you. "A pure bare going forth," says Tauler,[27] trying to describe the sensations of the self at this moment. "None," says Ruysbroeck, putting this same experience, this meek outstreaming of the bewildered spirit, into other language, "is sure of Eternal Life, unless he has died with his own attributes wholly into God."

It is unlikely that agreeable emotions will accompany this utter self-surrender; for everything will now seem to be taken from you, nothing given in exchange. But if you are able to make it, a mighty transformation will result. From the transitional plane of darkness, you will be reborn into another "world," another stage of realization: and find yourself, literally, to be other than you were before. Ascetic writers tell us that the essence of the change now effected consists in the fact that "God's *action* takes the place of man's *activity*"—that the surrendered self "does not act, but receives." By this they

---

27. Johannes Tauler (c. 1300–61), German Dominican preacher and mystic. (Eds.)

mean to describe, as well as our concrete language will permit, the new and vivid consciousness which now invades the contemplative; the sense which he has of being as it were helpless in the grasp of another Power, so utterly part of him, so completely different from him—so rich and various, so transfused with life and feeling, so urgent and so all-transcending—that he can only think of it as God. It is for this that the dimness and steadily increasing passivity of the stage of Quiet has been preparing him; and it is out of this willing quietude and ever-deepening obscurity that the new experiences come.

> *O night that didst lead thus,*
> *O night more lovely than the dawn of light,*
> *O night that broughtest us*
> *Lover to lover's sight—*
> *Lover with loved in marriage of delight,*

says St. John of the Cross[28] in the most wonderful of all mystical poems. "He who has had experience of this," says St. Teresa of the same stage of apprehension, "will understand it in some measure: but it cannot be more clearly described because what then takes place is so obscure. All I am able to say is, that the soul is represented as being close to God; and that there abides a conviction thereof so certain and strong, that it cannot possibly help believing so."

---

28. St. John of the Cross (1542–91), Carmelite priest and greatest of the Spanish mystic poets. (Eds.)

This sense, this conviction, which may be translated by the imagination into many different forms, is the substance of the greatest experiences and highest joys of the mystical saints. The intensity with which it is realized will depend upon the ardor, purity, and humility of the experiencing soul: but even those who feel it faintly are convinced by it forevermore. In some great and generous spirits, able to endure the terrific onslaught of Reality, it may even reach a vividness by which all other things are obliterated; and the self, utterly helpless under the inundations of this transcendent life force, passes into that simple state of consciousness which is called Ecstasy.

But you are not to be frightened by these special manifestations or to suppose that here the road is barred against you. Though these great spirits have as it were a genius for Reality, a susceptibility to supernal impressions, so far beyond your own small talent that there seems no link between you: yet you have, since you are human, a capacity for the Infinite too. With less intensity, less splendor, but with a certitude which no arguments will ever shake, this sense of the Living Fact, and of its mysterious contacts with and invasions of the human spirit, may assuredly be realized by you. This realization—sometimes felt under the symbols of personality, sometimes under those of an impersonal but life-giving Force, Light, Energy, or Heat—is the ruling character of the third phase of contemplation and the reward of that meek passivity, that "busy idleness" as the mystics sometimes call it, which you have been striving to attain. Sooner or later, if you are patient, it will come to you through the darkness: a mysterious contact, a clear certitude of intercourse and of possession—perhaps so gradual in its approach that the break, the change from the ever-deepening stillness and peace of the second phase, is hardly felt by you; perhaps, if your nature be ardent and unstable, with a sudden shattering violence, in a "storm of love."

In either case, the advent of this experience is incalculable, and completely outside your own control. So far, to use St. Teresa's well-known image, you have been watering the garden of your spirit by hand; a poor and laborious method, yet one in which there is a definite relation between effort and result. But now the watering can is taken from you, and you must depend upon the rain: more generous, more fruitful, than anything which your own efforts could manage, but, in its incalculable visitations, utterly beyond your control. Here all one can say is this: that if you acquiesce in the heroic demands which the spiritual life now makes upon you, if you let yourself go, eradicate the last traces of self-interest even of the most spiritual kind—then, you have established conditions under which the forces of the spiritual world can work on you, heightening your susceptibilities, deepening and purifying your attention, so that you are able to taste and feel more and more of the inexhaustible riches of Reality.

Thus dying to your own will, waiting for what is given, infused, you will presently find that a change in your apprehension has indeed taken place: and that those who said self-loss was the only way to realization taught no pious fiction but the truth. The highest contemplative experience to which you have yet attained has seemed above all else a still aware-ness. The cessation of your own striving, a resting upon and within the Absolute World—these were its main characteristics for your consciousness. But now, this Ocean of Being is no longer felt by you as an emptiness, a solitude without bourne. Suddenly you know it to be instinct with a movement and life too great for you to apprehend. You are thrilled by a mighty energy, uncontrolled by you, unsolicited by you: its higher vitality is poured into your soul. You enter upon an experience for which all the terms of power, thought, motion, even of love, are inade-quate: yet which contains within itself the only com-plete expression of all these things. Your strength is now literally made perfect in weakness: because of the completeness of your dependence, a fresh life is infused into you, such as your old separate existence never knew. Moreover, to that diffused and imper-sonal sense of the Infinite, in which you have dipped yourself, and which swallows up and completes all the ideas your mind has ever built up with the help of the categories of time and space, is now added the consciousness of a Living Fact which includes, tran-scends, completes all that you mean by the categories of personality and of life. Those ineffective, half-conscious attempts toward free action, clear appre-hension, true union, which we dignify by the names of will, thought, and love are now seen matched by an Absolute Will, Thought, and Love, instantly recognized by the contemplating spirit as the highest reality it yet has known, and evoking in it a passionate and a humble joy.

This unmistakable experience has been achieved by the mystics of every religion; and when we read their statements, we know that all are speaking of the same thing. None who have had it have ever been able to doubt its validity. It has always become for them the central fact, by which all other realities must be tested and graduated. It has brought to them the deep consciousness of sources of abundant life now made accessible to man; of the impact of a mighty energy, gentle, passionate, self-giving, creative, which they can only call Absolute Love. Sometimes they feel this strange life moving and stirring within them. Sometimes it seems to pursue, entice, and besiege them. In every case, they are the passive objects upon which it works. It is now another Power which seeks the separated spirit and demands it; which knocks at the closed door of the narrow personality; which penetrates the contemplative consciousness through and through, speaking, stirring, compelling it; which sometimes, by its secret irresistible pressure, wins even the most recalcitrant in spite of themselves. Sometimes this Power is felt as an impersonal force, the unifying cosmic energy, the in-drawing love which gathers all things into One; sometimes as a sudden access of vitality, a light and heat, enfolding and penetrating the self and making its languid life more vivid and more real; sometimes as a personal and friendly Presence which counsels and entreats the soul.

In each case, the mystics insist again that this is God; that here under these diverse manners the soul has immediate intercourse with Him. But we must remember that when they make this declaration, they are speaking from a plane of consciousness far above the ideas and images of popular religion and from a place which is beyond the judiciously adjusted horizon of philosophy. They mean by this word, not a notion, however august, but an experienced Fact so vivid, that against it the so-called facts of daily life look shadowy and insecure. They say that this Fact is "immanent," dwelling in, transfusing, and discoverable through every aspect of the universe, every movement of the game of life—as you have found in the first stage of contemplation. There you may hear its melody and discern its form. And further, that It is "transcendent"; in essence exceeding and including the sum of those glimpses and contacts which we obtain by self-mergence in life, and in Its simplest manifestations above and beyond anything to which reason can attain—"the Nameless Being, of Whom naught can be said." This you discovered to be true in the second stage. But in addition to this, they say also that this all-pervasive, all-changing, and yet changeless One, Whose melody is heard in all movement, and within Whose Being "the worlds are being told like beads," calls the human spirit to an immediate intercourse, a *unity,* a fruition, a divine give-and-take, for which the contradictory symbols of feeding, of touching, of marriage, of immersion, are all too poor; and which evokes in the fully conscious soul a passionate and a humble love. "He devours us and He feeds us!" exclaims Ruysbroeck. "Here," says St. Thomas Aquinas, "the soul in a wonderful and unspeakable manner both seizes and is seized upon, devours and is herself devoured, embraces and is violently embraced: and by the knot of love she unites herself with God, and is with Him as the Alone with the Alone."

The marvelous love poetry of mysticism, the rhapsodies which extol the spirit's Lover, Friend, Companion, Bridegroom; which describe the "deliberate speed, majestic instancy" of the Hound of Heaven chasing the separated soul, the onslaughts, demands, and caresses of this "stormy, generous, and unfathomable love"—all this is an attempt, often of course oblique and symbolic in method, to express and impart this transcendent secret, to describe that intense yet elusive state in which alone union with the living heart of Reality is possible. "How delicately Thou teachest love to me!" cries St. John of the Cross; and here indeed we find all the ardors of all earthly lovers justified by an imperishable Objective, which reveals Itself in all things that we truly love, and beyond all these things both seeks us and compels us, "giving more than we can take and asking more than we can pay."

You do not, you never will, know *what* this Objective is: for as Dionysius teaches, "if any one saw God and understood what he saw, then it was not God that he saw, but something that belongs to Him." But you do know now that it exists, with an intensity which makes all other existences unreal, save insofar as they participate in this one Fact. "Some contemplate the Formless, and others meditate on Form: but the wise man knows that Brahma is beyond both." As you yield yourself more and more completely to the impulses of this intimate yet unseizable Presence, so much the sweeter and stronger—so much the more constant and steady—will your intercourse with it become. The imperfect music of your adoration will be answered and reinforced by another music, gentle, deep, and strange; your outgoing movement, the stretching forth of your desire from yourself to something other, will be answered by a movement, a stirring, within you yet not conditioned by you. The wonder and variety of this intercourse is never ending. It includes in its sweep every phase of human love and self-devotion, all beauty and all power, all suffering and effort, all gentleness and rapture: here found in synthesis. Going forth into the bareness and darkness of this unwalled world of high contemplation, you there find stored for you, and at last made real, all the highest values, all the dearest and noblest experiences of the world of growth and change.

You see now what it is that you have been doing in the course of your mystical development. As your narrow heart stretched to a wider sympathy with life, you have been surrendering progressively to larger and larger existences, more and more complete realities: have been learning to know them, to share their very being, through the magic of disinterested love. First, the manifested, flowing, evolving life of multiplicity: felt by you in its wonder and wholeness, once you learned to yield yourself to its rhythms, received in simplicity the undistorted messages of sense. Then, the actual unchanging ground of life, the eternal and unconditioned Whole, transcending all succession: a world inaccessible alike to senses and intelligence, but felt—vaguely, darkly, yet intensely—by the quiet and surrendered consciousness. But now you are solicited, whether you will or no, by a greater Reality, the final inclusive Fact, the Unmeasured Love, which "is through all things everlastingly": and yielding yourself to it, receiving and responding to its obscure yet ardent communications, you pass beyond the cosmic experience to the personal encounter, the simple yet utterly inexpressible union of the soul with its God.

And this threefold union with Reality, as your attention is focused now on one aspect, now on another, of its rich simplicity, will be actualized by you in many different ways: for you are not to suppose that an unchanging barren ecstasy is now to characterize your inner life. Though the sense of your own dwelling within the Eternal transfuses and illuminates it, the sense of your own necessary efforts, a perpetual renewal of contact with the Spiritual World, a perpetual self-donation, shall animate it too. When the greater love overwhelms the lesser, and your small self-consciousness is lost in the consciousness of the Whole, it will be felt as an intense stillness, a quiet fruition of Reality. Then, your very selfhood seems to cease, as it does in all your moments of great passion; and you are "satisfied and overflowing, and with Him beyond yourself eternally fulfilled." Again, when your own necessary activity comes into the foreground, your small energetic love perpetually pressing to deeper and deeper realization—"tasting through and through, and seeking through and through, the fathomless ground" of the Infinite and Eternal—it seems rather a perpetually renewed encounter than a final achievement. Since you are a child of Time as well as of Eternity, such effort and satisfaction, active and passive love are both needed by you, if your whole life is to be brought into union with the inconceivably rich yet simple One in Whom these apparent opposites are harmonized. Therefore, seeking and finding, work and rest, conflict and peace, feeding on God and self-immersion in God, spiritual marriage and spiritual death—these contradictory images are all wanted, if we are to represent the changing moods of the living, growing human spirit, the diverse aspects under which it realizes the simple fact of its intercourse with the Divine.

Each new stage achieved in the mystical development of the spirit has meant, not the leaving behind of the previous stages, but an adding on to them: an ever-greater extension of experience, and enrichment of personality. So that the total result of this change, this steady growth of your transcendental self, is not an impoverishment of the sense-life in the supposed interests of the supersensual, but the addition to it of another life—a huge widening and deepening of the field over which your attention can play. Sometimes the mature contemplative consciousness narrows to an intense point of feeling, in which it seems indeed "alone with the Alone":

sometimes it spreads to a vast apprehension of the Universal Life, or perceives the common things of sense aflame with God. It moves easily and with no sense of incongruity from hours of close personal communion with its Friend and Lover to self-loss in the "deep yet dazzling darkness" of the Divine Abyss; or, reentering that living world of change which the first form of contemplation disclosed to it, passes beyond those discrete manifestations of Reality to realize the Whole which dwells in and inspires every part. Thus ascending to the mysterious fruition of that Reality which is beyond image, and descending again to the loving contemplation and service of all struggling growing things, it now finds and adores everywhere—in the sky and the nest, the soul and the void—one Energetic Love which "is measureless, since it is all that exists," and of which the patient up-climb of the individual soul, the passionate outpouring of the Divine Mind, form the completing opposites.

Chapter X

THE MYSTICAL LIFE

And here the practical man, who has been strangely silent during the last stages of our discourse, shakes himself like a terrier which has achieved dry land again after a bath, and asks once more, with a certain explosive violence, his dear old question, "What is the *use* of all this?"

"You have introduced me," he says further, "to some curious states of consciousness, interesting enough in their way; and to a lot of peculiar emotions, many of which are no doubt most valuable to poets and so on. But it is all so remote from daily life. How is it going to fit in with ordinary existence? How, above all, is it all going to help *me*?"

Well, put upon its lowest plane, this new way of attending to life—this deepening and widening of outlook—may at least be as helpful to you as many things to which you have unhesitatingly consecrated much time and diligence in the past: your long journeys to new countries, for instance, or long hours spent in acquiring new "facts," relabeling old experiences, gaining skill in new arts and games. These, it is true, were quite worth the effort expended on them: for they gave you, in exchange for your labor and attention, a fresh view of certain fragmentary things, a new point of contact with the rich world of possibilities, a tiny enlargement of your universe in one direction or another. Your love and patient study of nature, art, science, politics, business—even of sport—repaid you thus. But I have offered you, in exchange for a meek and industrious attention to another aspect of the world, hitherto somewhat neglected by you, an enlargement which shall include and transcend all these, and be conditioned only by the perfection of your generosity, courage, and surrender.

Nor are you to suppose that this enlargement will be limited to certain new spiritual perceptions, which the art of contemplation has made possible for you: that it will merely draw the curtain from a window out of which you have never looked. This new wide world is not to be for you something seen, but something lived in: and you—since man is a creature of responses—will insensibly change under its influence, growing up into a more perfect conformity with it. Living in this atmosphere of Reality, you will, in fact, yourself become more real. Hence, if you accept in a spirit of trust the suggestions which have been made to you—and I acknowledge that here at the beginning an attitude of faith is essential—and if you practice with diligence the arts which I have described: then, sooner or later, you will inevitably find yourself deeply and permanently changed by them—will perceive that you have become a "new man." Not merely have you acquired new powers of perception and new ideas of Reality; but a quiet and complete transformation, a strengthening and maturing of your personality, has taken place.

You are still, it is true, living the ordinary life of the body. You are immersed in the stream of duration, a part of the human, the social, the national group. The emotions, instincts, needs of that group affect you. Your changing scrap of vitality contributes to its corporate life, and contributes the more effectively since a new, intuitive sympathy has now made its interests your own. Because of that corporate life, transfusing you, giving to you and taking from you—conditioning you as it does in countless oblique and unapparent ways—you are still compelled to react to many suggestions which you are no longer able to respect: controlled, to the last moment of your bodily existence and perhaps afterward, by habit, custom, the good old average way of misunderstanding the world. To this extent, the crowd spirit has you in its grasp.

Yet in spite of all this, you are now released from that crowd's tyrannically overwhelming consciousness as you never were before. You feel yourself now a separate vivid entity, a real, whole man: dependent on the Whole, and gladly so dependent, yet within that Whole a free self-governing thing. Perhaps you always fancied that your will was free—that you were actually, as you sometimes said, the "captain of your soul." If so, this was merely one among the many illusions which supported your old, enslaved career. As a matter of fact, you were driven along a road, unaware of anything that lay beyond the hedges, pressed on every side by other members of the flock, getting perhaps a certain satisfaction out of the deep warm stir of the collective life, but igno-

rant of your destination, and with your personal initiative limited to the snatching of grass as you went
along, the pushing of your way to the softer side of
the track. These operations made up together that
which you called Success. But now, because you
have achieved a certain power of gathering yourself
together, perceiving yourself as a person, a spirit,
and observing your relation with these other individual lives—because too, hearing now and again
the mysterious piping of the Shepherd, you realize
your own perpetual forward movement and that of
the flock, in its relation to that living guide—you
have a far deeper, truer knowledge than ever before
both of the general and the individual existence; and
so are able to handle life with a surer hand.

Do not suppose from this that your new career is
to be perpetually supported by agreeable spiritual
contacts, or occupy itself in the mild contemplation
of the great world through which you move. True, it
is said of the Shepherd that he carries the lambs in
his bosom: but the sheep are expected to walk, and
put up with the inequalities of the road, the bunts
and blunders of the flock. It is to vigor rather than to
comfort that you are called. Since the transcendental
aspect of your being has been brought into focus
you are now raised out of the mere push forward,
the blind passage through time of the flock, into a
position of creative responsibility. You are aware of
personal correspondences with the Shepherd. You
correspond, too, with a larger, deeper, broader world.
The sky and the hedges, the wide lands through
which you are moving, the corporate character and

meaning of the group to which you belong—all these are now within the circle of your consciousness; and each little event, each separate demand or invitation which comes to you, is now seen in a truer proportion, because you bring to it your awareness of the Whole. Your journey ceases to be an automatic progress, and takes on some of the characters of a free act: for "things" are now under you, you are no longer under them.

You will hardly deny that this is a practical gain: that this widening and deepening of the range over which your powers of perception work makes you more of a man than you were before, and thus adds to rather than subtracts from your total practical efficiency. It is indeed only when he reaches these levels, and feels within himself this creative freedom—this full actualization of himself—on the one hand: on the other hand the sense of a world order, a love and an energy on which he depends and with whose interests he is now at one, that man becomes fully human, capable of living the real life of Eternity in the midst of the world of time.

And what, when you have come to it, do you suppose to be your own function in this vast twofold scheme? Is it for nothing, do you think, that you are thus a meeting place of two orders? Surely it is your business, so far as you may, to express in action something of the real character of that universe within which you now know yourself to live? Artists, aware of a more vivid and more beautiful world than other men, are always driven by their love and enthusiasm to try and express, bring into direct manifestation, those deeper significances of form, sound, rhythm, which they have been able to apprehend: and, doing this, they taste deeper and deeper truths, make ever-closer unions with the Real. For them, the duty of creation is tightly bound up with the gift of love. In their passionate outflowing to the universe which offers itself under one of its many aspects to their adoration, that other-worldly fruition of beauty is always followed, balanced, completed, by a this-world impulse to creation: a desire to fix within the time-order, and share with other men, the vision by which they were possessed. Each one, thus bringing new aspects of beauty, new ways of seeing and hearing within the reach of the race, does something to amend the sorry universe of common sense, the more hideous universe of greed, and redeem his fellows from their old, slack servitude to a lower range of significances. It is in action, then, that these find their truest and safest point of insertion into the living, active world of Reality: in sharing and furthering its work of manifestation they know its secrets best. For them contemplation and action are not opposites, but two interdependent forms of a life that is *one*—a life that rushes out to a passionate communion with the true and beautiful, only that it may draw from this direct experience of Reality a new intensity wherewith to handle the world of things and remake it, or at least some little bit of it, "nearer to the heart's desire."

Again, the great mystics tell us that the "vision of God in His own light"—the direct contact of the soul's substance with the Absolute—to which awful experience you drew as near as the quality of your spirit would permit in the third degree of contemplation, is the prelude, not to a further revelation of the eternal order given to you, but to an utter change, a vivid life springing up within you, which they sometimes call the "transforming union" or the "birth of the Son in the soul." By this they mean that the spark of spiritual stuff, that high special power or character of human nature, by which you first desired, then tended to, then achieved contact with Reality, is as it were fertilized by this profound communion with its origin; becomes strong and vigorous, invades and transmutes the whole personality, and makes of it, not a "dreamy mystic" but an active and impassioned servant of the Eternal Wisdom.

So that when these full-grown, fully vital mystics try to tell us about the life they have achieved, it is always an intensely active life that they describe. They say, not that they "dwell in restful fruition," though the deep and joyous knowledge of this, perhaps too the perpetual longing for an utter self-loss in it, is always possessed by them—but that they "go up *and down* the ladder of contemplation." They stretch up toward the Point, the unique Reality to which all the intricate and many-colored lines of life flow, and in which they are merged; and rush out toward those various lives in a passion of active love and service. This double activity, this swinging between rest and work—this alone, they say, is truly the life of man; because this alone represents on human levels something of that inexhaustibly rich yet simple life, "ever active yet ever at rest," which they find in God. When he gets to this, then man has indeed actualized his union with Reality; because then he is a part of the perpetual creative act, the eternal generation of the Divine thought and love. Therefore contemplation, even at its highest, dearest, and most intimate, is not to be for you an end in itself. It shall only be truly yours when it impels you to action: when the double movement of Transcendent Love, drawing inward to unity and fruition, and rushing out again to creative acts, is realized in you. You are to be a living, ardent tool with which the Supreme Artist works: one of the instruments of His self-manifestation, the perpetual process by which His Reality is brought into concrete expression.

Now the expression of vision, of reality, of beauty, at an artist's hands—the creation of new life in all forms—has two factors: the living molding creative spirit, and the material in which it works. Between these two there is inevitably a difference of tension. The material is at best inert, and merely patient of the informing idea; at worst, directly recalcitrant to it. Hence, according to the balance of these two factors, the amount of resistance offered by stuff to tool, a greater or less energy must be expended, greater or less perfection of result will be achieved. You, accepting the wide deep universe of the mystic, and the responsibilities that go with it, have by this act taken sides once and for all with creative spirit: with the higher tension, the unrelaxed effort, the passion for a better, intenser, and more significant life. The adoration to which you are vowed is not an affair of red hassocks and authorized hymn books; but a burning and consuming fire. You will find, then, that the world, going its own gait, busily occupied with its own system of correspondences—yielding to every gust of passion, intent on the satisfaction of greed, the struggle for comfort or for power—will oppose your new eagerness; perhaps with violence, but more probably with the exasperating calmness of a heavy animal which refuses to get up. If your new life is worth anything, it will flame to sharper power when it strikes against this dogged inertness of things: for you need resistances on which to act. "The road to a Yea lies through a Nay," and righteous warfare is the only way to a living and a lasting peace.

Further, you will observe more and more clearly, that the stuff of your external world, the method and machinery of the common life, is not merely passively but actively inconsistent with your sharp interior vision of truth. The heavy animal is diseased as well as indolent. All man's perverse ways of seeing his universe, all the perverse and hideous acts which have sprung from them—these have set up reactions, have produced deep disorders in the world of things. Man is free, and holds the keys of hell as well as the keys of heaven. Within the love-driven universe which you have learned to see as a whole, you will therefore find egotism, rebellion, meanness, brutality, squalor: the work of separated selves whose energies are set athwart the stream.

But every aspect of life, however falsely imagined, can still be "saved," turned to the purposes of Reality: for "all-thing hath the being by the love of God." Its oppositions are no part of its realness; and therefore they can be overcome. Is there not here, then, abundance of practical work for you to do; work which is the direct outcome of your mystical experience? Are there not here, as the French proverb has it, plenty of cats for you to comb? And isn't it just here, in the new foothold it gives you, the new clear vision and certitude—in its noble, serious, and invulnerable faith—that mysticism is "useful," even for the most scientific of social reformers, the most belligerent of politicians, the least sentimental of philanthropists?

To "bring Eternity into Time," the "invisible into concrete expression"; to "be to the Eternal Goodness what his own hand is to a man"—these are the plainly expressed desires of all the great mystics. One and all, they demand earnest and deliberate action, the insertion of the purified and ardent will into the world of things. The mystics are artists; and the stuff in which they work is most often human life. They want to heal the disharmony between the actual and the real: and since, in the white-hot radiance of that faith, hope, and charity which burns in them, they discern such a reconciliation to be possible, they are able to work for it with a singleness of purpose and an invincible optimism denied to other men. This was the instinct which drove St. Francis of Assisi to the practical experience of that poverty which he recognized as the highest wisdom;

St. Catherine of Siena[29] from contemplation to politics; Joan of Arc to the salvation of France; St. Teresa to the formation of an ideal religious family; [George] Fox to the proclaiming of a world religion in which all men should be guided by the Inner Light; Florence Nightingale to battle with officials, vermin, dirt, and disease in the soldiers' hospitals; Octavia Hill[30] to make in London slums something a little nearer "the shadows of the angels' houses" than that which the practical landlord usually provides.

All these have felt sure that a great part in the drama of creation has been given to the free spirit of man: that bit by bit, through and by him, the scattered worlds of love and thought and action shall be realized again as one. It is for those who have found the thread on which those worlds are strung to bring this knowledge out of the hiddenness, to use it, as the old alchemists declared that they could use their tincture, to transmute all baser metals into gold.

So here is your vocation set out: a vocation so various in its opportunities, that you can hardly fail to find something to do. It is your business to actualize within the world of time and space—perhaps by great endeavors in the field of heroic action, perhaps only by small ones in field and market, tram and tube, office and drawing room, in the perpetual give

---

29. St. Catherine of Siena (1347–80), virgin, mystic, and Dominican nun. (Eds.)

30. Octavia Hill (1838–1912), a founder of Britain's National Trust and believer in open spaces for all. (Eds.)

and take of the common life—that more real life, that holy creative energy, which this world manifests as a whole but indifferently. You shall work for mercy, order, beauty, significance: shall mend where you find things broken, make where you find the need. *"Adoro te devote, latens Deitas,"* said St. Thomas in his great mystical hymn: and the practical side of that adoration consists in the bringing of the Real Presence from its hiddenness, and exhibiting it before the eyes of other men. Hitherto you have not been very active in this matter: yet it is the purpose for which you exist, and your contemplative consciousness, if you educate it, will soon make this fact clear to you. The teeming life of nature has yielded up to your loving attention many sacramental images of Reality: seen in the light of charity, it is far more sacred and significant than you supposed. What about *your* life? Is that a theophany too? "Each oak doth cry I AM," says Vaughan.[31] Do you proclaim by your existence the grandeur, the beauty, the intensity, the living wonder of that Eternal Reality within which, at this moment, you stand? Do your hours of contemplation and of action harmonize?

If they did harmonize—if everybody's did— then, by these individual adjustments the complete group consciousness of humanity would be changed, brought back into conformity with the Transcendent; and the spiritual world would be actualized

---

31. Henry Vaughan (1622–95), English metaphysical and religious poet. (Eds.)

within the temporal order at last. Then, that world of false imagination, senseless conflicts, and sham values, into which our children are now born, would be annihilated. The whole race, not merely a few of its noblest, most clear-sighted spirits, would be "in union with God"; and men, transfused by His light and heat, direct and willing agents of His Pure Activity, would achieve that completeness of life which the mystics dare to call "deification." This is the substance of that redemption of the world, which all religions proclaim or demand: the consummation which is crudely imagined in the Apocalyptic dreams of the prophets and seers. It is the true incarnation of the Divine Wisdom: and you must learn to see with Paul the pains and disorders of creation—your own pains, efforts, and difficulties too—as incidents in the travail of that royal birth. Patriots have sometimes been asked to "think imperially." Mystics are asked to think celestially; and this, not when considering the things usually called spiritual, but when dealing with the concrete accidents, the evil and sadness, the cruelty, failure, and degeneration of life.

So, what is being offered to you is not merely a choice among new states of consciousness, new emotional experiences—though these are indeed involved in it—but, above all else, a larger and intenser life, a career, a total consecration to the interests of the Real. This life shall not be abstract and dreamy, made up, as some imagine, of negations. It shall be violently practical and affirmative, giving scope for a limitless activity of will, heart, and mind working within the rhythms of the Divine Idea. It shall cost much, making perpetual demands on your loyalty, trust, and self-sacrifice: proving now the need and the worth of that training in renunciation which was forced on you at the beginning of your interior life. It shall be both deep and wide, embracing in its span all those aspects of Reality which the gradual extension of your contemplative powers has disclosed to you: making "the inner and outer worlds to be indivisibly One." And because the emphasis is now forever shifted from the accidents to the substance of life, it will matter little where and how this career is actualized—whether in convent or factory, study or battlefield, multitude or solitude, sickness or strength. These fluctuations of circumstance will no longer dominate you, since "it is Love that payeth for all."

Yet by all this it is not meant that the opening up of the universe, the vivid consciousness of a living Reality and your relation with it, which came to you in contemplation, will necessarily be a constant or a governable feature of your experience. Even under the most favorable circumstances, you shall and must move easily and frequently between that spiritual fruition and active work in the world of men. Often enough it will slip from you utterly; often your most diligent effort will fail to recapture it, and only its fragrance will remain. The more intense those contacts have been, the more terrible will be your hunger and desolation when they are thus withdrawn: for increase of susceptibility means more pain as well as more pleasure, as every artist knows. But you will find in all that happens to you, all that opposes and grieves you—even in those inevitable hours of darkness when the doors of true perception seem to close, and the cruel tangles of the world are all that you can discern—an inward sense of security which will never cease. All the waves that buffet you about, shaking sometimes the strongest faith and hope, are yet parts and aspects of one Ocean. Did they wreck you utterly, that Ocean would receive you; and there you would find, overwhelming and transfusing you, the unfathomable Substance of all life and joy. Whether you realize it in its personal or impersonal manifestation, the universe is now friendly to you; and as he is a suspicious and unworthy lover who asks every day for renewed demonstrations of love, so you do not demand from it perpetual reassurances. It is enough, that once it showed you its heart. A link of love now binds you to it forevermore: in spite of derelictions, in spite of darkness and suffering, your will is harmonized with the Will that informs the Whole.

We said, at the beginning of this discussion, that mysticism was the art of union with Reality: that it was, above all else, a Science of Love. Hence, the condition to which it looks forward and toward which the soul of the contemplative has been stretching out, is a condition of *being,* not of *seeing.* As the bodily senses have been produced under pressure of man's physical environment, and their true aim is not the enhancement of his pleasure or his knowledge, but a perfecting of his adjustment to those aspects of the natural world which concern him—so the use and meaning of the spiritual senses are strictly practical too. These, when developed by a suitable training, reveal to man a certain measure of Reality: not in order that he may gaze upon it, but in order that he may react to it, learn to live in, with, for it, growing and stretching into more perfect harmony with the Eternal Order, until at last, like the blessed ones of Dante's vision, the clearness of his flame responds to the unspeakable radiance of the Enkindling Light.

Abba

FOR B.B.G.

Chapter I
INTRODUCTORY

Prayer is the substance of eternal life. It gives back to man, insofar as he is willing to live to capacity—that is to say, to give love and suffer pain—the beatitude without which he is incomplete; for it sets going, deepens, and at last perfects that mutual indwelling of two orders which redeems us from unreality, and in which the creative process reaches its goal. There is, as Bremond[1] has said, even in the poorest and crudest prayer "a touch of Pentecost." It awaits and expects the action of the Spirit, acknowledges the most mysterious and yet the most certain reality of our experience; the intercourse of the Transcendent God with fugitive man, and of fugitive man with the Transcendent God. Yet all our attempts to describe this mysterious reality are like the scientists' attempts to describe the universe; at worst diagrammatic, at best symbolic and allusive. It eludes definition, refuses to be caught in the meshes of the mind. We cannot say of it on God's side, "Lo! there the begin-

---

1. Henri Bremond (1865–1933), French spiritual writer. Ordained a Jesuit priest in 1892; influenced by John Henry Cardinal Newman. Left Jesuits in 1904 to become a secular priest. His most famous work was the six-volume *L'histoire littéraire du sentiment religieux en France.* (Eds.)

ning"; nor on man's side, "Lo! here"; because it comes not with observation, but emerges unperceived from that deep ground of being where we do not know ourselves apart from Him. There, beyond thought, the pressure and invitation of God is experienced by the creature, and thence there filters into consciousness some response to the Unseen; an act of loving attention, a submission, a supplication. Here is the beginning of prayer, and hence it spreads to include at last every level of our being, every aspect of our existence, and bring into conscious expression its fundamental relation with God.

This is a conception of prayer which we easily forget; for the cheap fussiness of the anthropocentric life has even invaded our religion. There too, we prefer to live upon the surface and ignore the deeps. We seldom pause for that awed recognition of pure Being, so steadying and refreshing to the soul, which is the raw material of the interior life. Yet the true growth and development of humanity seems to depend on this constant reorientation toward the Holy, this deep thrust of the spirit to the unchanging sources of its life. When a seed germinates, first the radicle pushes down into the nourishing earth; its delicate exploring tip penetrates that dense and hidden world, seeking and finding food. After that, the plumule unfolds and emerges into the light and air. Thus it should be with the spirit of man. The small seed of transcendental life in him, which the vicissitudes of circumstance will feed, maim, or kill, according to the dispositions of the soul, must thrust its rootlet down into the world of spirit before it pushes its plumule up. Prayer must precede action. A deep adherence in our ground to absolute Beauty and Love is the only condition under which we can manifest beauty and love, and so redeem the world's ugliness and sin. But we have come to believe that we can ignore this spiritual imperative, have the shoot without the root; Christian action without Christian contemplation, the fruitful ideology without contact with the Idea. The parable of the Sower is there to warn us of the inevitable result; and indeed the whole of the New Testament, once we have discarded our utilitarian prejudices and learned to look at it with innocence of eye, decisively announces the priority of the spiritual, the mysterious greatness of prayer.

Christ, whose earthly life was both a correction and a completion of human life, taught above all else, by example as well as precept, this supreme art and privilege of the borderland creature. For Him, man was a being set in the world of succession and subject to its griefs and limitations; yet able in his prayer to move out to the very frontiers of that world, to lay hold on the Eternal and experience another level of life. How different such a doctrine and practice were from those of his own or any other time, is shown by the demand of the disciples who had witnessed His nights of solitary prayer in the hills: "Teach us *how* to pray." Those who asked this were good and pious Jews, who already accepted the worship of the Name and practice of daily prayer as a normal part of life. But now they realized how far beyond these orderly acts of worship and petition was that living intercourse with the living Father, which conditioned every moment of Christ's life; His link with the Unseen Reality from which He came and the source of His power in the world to which He was sent. Here for the first time they saw prayer, not as an ordered action, or a religious duty, not even an experience; but as a vital relation between man in his wholeness and the Being of God. Here was one who knew in the full and deep sense *how* to pray; and in the light of His practice, they perceived the poverty and unreality of their own.

The New Testament has preserved for us, in our Lord's reply to His followers, a complete description of what Christian prayer should be; its character and objective; its balance and proportion; its quality and tone. As we explore this description and try to realize all that is implied in it, we find the whole world of prayer, its immense demands and immense possibilities, opening before us. Yet in accordance with that steady hold on history, that deep respect for the tradition within which He appeared, which marks the whole of Christ's teaching, the description was given—as the answer to those who asked for the secret of Eternal Life was given—in words which were already familiar to the askers: in seven linked phrases which were a part of Jewish prayer, and can be traced to their origin in the Old Testament. It is as if we went to a saint and asked him to teach us to pray, and he replied by reciting the Quinquagesima

Collect.[2] We can imagine the disappointment of the disciples—"We knew all this before!" The answer to this objection is the same as the answer to the Lawyer: this *do* and you shall live. You already have all the information. Invest it with realism, translate it into action: phrases into facts, theology into religion. I am not giving you a set formula for repetition, but seven complementary pictures of the one life of prayer.

There is a drawing by William Blake, called "The Prayer of the Infant Jesus," which seems to show us the response by anticipation to the disciples' petition "Teach us how to pray." The Child who kneels upon the bed in the center of the picture is already a Master of prayer. The radiance of the Uncreated Light, breaking the surrounding darkness, falls upon Him. In His tiny figure, perfect in poise and happiness, human nature—and in human nature all creation—is brought into filial relation with God: a whole poured out in love toward a Whole. Round Him are His pupils visible and invisible; for Love incarnate has its own lessons to teach, even to discarnate spirits. The angels, humbled and exultant, kneel in awe before the mystery of the Word, uttering from within His own creation the praise of the ineffable Name. Behind, with closed eyes and folded hands, devout and recollected, are

---

2. A short liturgical prayer said the Sunday before Ash Wednesday. (Eds.)

the earthly forms of Mary and Joseph. Above them their immortal spirits, already citizens of the world of supernatural prayer, bend their piercing gaze upon this Child, who knits together the worship of heaven and earth. On all, men and angels, lies a great silence in which the Divine Wisdom begins, from within humanity, His redeeming work.

If, looking at this picture, we consider the seven clauses of the Lord's Prayer, we shall find here the link which binds them all together; so that they become seven moments in a single act of communion, seven doors opening upon "the world that is unwalled." For these seven clauses represent seven fundamental characters of the one indivisible relation between the spirit of man and the Eternal God; they are seven lessons in prayer, forming together a complete direction for the conduct of our inner life. We begin to realize this, when we consider each separately, and see something of what each of them involves.

(1) *Our Father which art in heaven:* the sublime invocation which establishes our status before God, not merely as His creatures and slaves but as His children. We are the sons and daughters of the Eternal Perfect, inheritors of the Abiding; we have in us the spark of absolute life.

(2) *Hallowed be Thy Name:* selfless adoration, awestruck worship as the ruling temper of our life and all we do.

(3) *Thy Kingdom come:* devoted and eager cooperation with His transforming and redeeming action;

the defeat of evil and the triumph of love as the first object of our prayer.

(4) *Thy Will be done:* active self-abandonment to the mysterious purposes and methods of God, and complete subordination to His design, as the perpetual disposition of the soul.

(5) *Give us this day our daily bread:* confident dependence on God for all the necessities of life. "Without thee I cannot live."

(6) *And forgive us our trespasses,* our debts—the too much and the too little—the major types of disharmony with love: the prayer of filial penitence.

(7) *Lead us not into temptation:* the acknowledgment of our creaturely weakness and trust in His prevenient care.

And then the great affirmation which embraces and justifies our faith, hope, and charity: "*Thine* is the Kingdom, the Power, and the Glory." We ask this of you, for only you can do it: no lesser power, no lesser love, will suffice.

Lover of souls, Great God, I look to thee.

It is too often supposed that when our Lord said, "In this manner pray ye," He meant not "these are the right dispositions and longings, the fundamental acts of every soul that prays," but "this is the form of words which, above all others, Christians are required to repeat." As a consequence this is the prayer in which, with an almost incredible stupidity, they have found the material of those vain repetitions which He has specially condemned. Again and again in public and private devotion the Lord's Prayer is taken on hurried lips, and recited at a pace which makes impossible any realization of its tremendous claims and profound demands. Far better than this cheapening of the awful power of prayer was the practice of the old woman described by St. Teresa, who spent an hour over the first two words, absorbed in reverence and love.

It is true, of course, that this pattern in its verbal form, its obvious and surface meaning, is far too familiar to us. Rapid and frequent repetition has reduced it to a formula. We are no longer conscious of its mysterious beauty and easily assume that we have long ago exhausted its inexhaustible significance. The result of this persistent error has been to limit our understanding of the great linked truths which are here given to us; to harden their edges, and turn an instruction which sets up a standard for each of the seven elements of prayer, and was intended to govern our whole life toward God, into a set form of universal obligation.

This is a sovereign instance of that spiritual stupidity with which we treat the "awful and mysterious truths" religion reveals to us; truths of which Coleridge has rightly said, that they are commonly "considered so true as to lose all the powers of truth, and lie bedridden in the dormitory of the soul."[3] But

---

3. Samuel Taylor Coleridge (1772–1834), *Table Talk*, 28th June, 1834.

when we "center down," as Quakers say, from the surface of human life to its deeps, and rouse those sleeping truths and take them with us, and ask what they look like there—in the secret place where the soul is alone with God and knows its need of God—then, all looks different. These great declarations disclose their intensity of life, their absolute quality; as a work of art which has hung respected and unloved in a public gallery glows with new meaning when we bring it into the home or the sanctuary for which it was really made. Seen thus, the Paternoster reminds us how rich and various, how deeply rooted in the Supernatural, the Christian life is or should be, moving from awestruck worship to homely confidence, and yet one: how utterly it depends on God, yet how searching is the demand it makes on man. "Every just man," says [Francisco de] Osuna, "needs the seven things for which this prayer—or this scheme of prayer—asks."[4] Taken together they cover all the realities of our situation, at once beset by nature and cherished by grace: establishing Christian prayer as a relation between wholes, between man in his completeness and God who is all.

And we note their order and proportion. First, four clauses entirely concerned with our relation to God; then three concerned with our human situation and needs. Four hinge on the First Commandment, three hinge on the Second. Man's twisted, thwarted, and embittered nature, his state of sin, his

---

4. *The Third Spiritual Alphabet,* Treatise 13.

sufferings, helplessness, and need, do not stand in
the foreground; but the splendor and beauty of God,
demanding a self-oblivion so complete that it transforms suffering, and blots out even the memory of
sin. We begin with a sublime yet intimate invocation
of Reality, which plunges us at once into the very
ground of the Universe and claims kinship with the
enfolding mystery. Abba, Father. The Infinite God
is the Father of my soul. We end by the abject confession of our dependence and need of guidance: of a
rescue and support coming to our help right down
in the jungle of life. Following the path of the Word
Incarnate, this prayer begins on the summits of spiritual experience and comes steadily down from
the Infinite to the finite, from the Spaceless to the little space on which we stand. Here we find all the
strange mixed experience of man, overruled by the
unchanging glory and charity of God.

Chapter II
THE FATHER

The crowds who followed Christ hoping for healing or counsel did not ask Him to teach them how to pray; nor did He give this prayer to them. It is not for those who want religion to be helpful, who seek after signs; those who expect it to solve their political problems and cure their diseases, but are not prepared to share its cost. He gave it to those whom He was going to incorporate into His rescuing system, use in His ministry; the sons of the Kingdom, self-given to the creative purposes of God. "*Thou* when thou prayest . . . pray ye on this manner." It is the prayer of those "sent forth" to declare the Kingdom, whom the world will hate, whose unpopularity with man will be in proportion to their loyalty to God; the apostles of the Perfect in whom, if they are true to their vocation, the Spirit of the Father will speak. The disciples sent out to do Christ's work were to depend on prayer, an unbroken communion with the Eternal; and this is the sort of prayer on which they were to depend. We therefore, when we dare to use it, offer ourselves by implication as their fellow workers for the Kingdom; for it supposes and requires an unconditional and filial devotion to the interests of God. Those who use the prayer must pray from the Cross.

In other words, this is essentially the prayer of the living Church, the supernatural society of God's children, the dedicated Body. It is addressed, not to Christ, who indwells and rules that dedicated Body, but to the Absolute God whom He reveals to men. "Because ye are sons, God sent forth the spirit of His Son into our hearts, crying Abba, Father."[5] By the free action of the Eternal Charity man has been lifted up from creation, and made capable of this word. The Incarnate Wisdom prays with and in us; and our worship as His must look beyond the distractions of the contingent to the eternal Beauty and Truth. In His prayer we seem to discern the perfect working of that *"intellectus purus et aequus"* of which Bacon said that it is "never distracted by the particulars and never lost in the contemplation of the entirety."

Yet on the other hand it is Man, haunted by sin, kept in perpetual tension between the pull of heaven and the pull of earth, the victim of the very desires that he repudiates and the distracted citizen of a universe which he cannot comprehend, who takes this word on his lips, and puts filial trust and filial adoration at the heart of his spiritual life. Only insofar as he is gathered into this relationship of worship, confidence, and love does he realize and express his shortcomings and his guilt. So the theme of the first movement of Christian prayer is the Glory of the Father, the shining forth of the Shekinah; and the

---

5. Gal. 4, 6.

straightening out of our deformed world so that it matches the "pattern in heaven," the unmanifest Creative design. But the theme of the second movement, with its humble petition for the support of the Unchanging Spirit in our ever-changing life, is weak and limited man, as he is now; his needs, his errors, his fears. Men have three wants, which only God can satisfy. They need food, for they are weak and dependent. They need forgiveness, for they are sinful. They need guidance, for they are puzzled. Give—Forgive—Lead—Deliver. All their prayer can be reduced to the loving adoration of the Father and the confident demand for His help.

"Our Father, which art in heaven." We are the children of God and therefore inheritors of heaven. Here is the source alike of our hope and our penitence; the standard which confounds us, the essence of religion, the whole of prayer. "Heaven is God and God is in my soul," said Elisabeth de la Trinité.[6] It is a statement of fact, which takes us clean away from the world of religious problems and consolations, the world of self-interested worries and strivings, and discloses the infinite span and unfathomable depth of that supernatural world in which we really live. From our distorted life "unquieted with dreads, bounden with cares, busied with vanities, vexed with temptations" [7] the soul in its prayer

---

6. Carmelite nun (1880–1906). (Eds.)

7. Thomas à Kempis, *The Imitation of Christ,* Bk. III, cap. 48.

reaches out to center its trust on the Eternal, the existent.

In those rare glimpses of Christ's own life of prayer which the Gospels vouchsafe to us, we always notice the perpetual reference to the unseen Father, so much more vividly present to Him than anything that is seen. Behind that daily life into which He entered so generously, filled as it was with constant appeals to His practical pity and help, there is ever the sense of that strong and tranquil Presence, ordering all things and bringing them to their appointed end; not with a rigid and mechanical precision, but with the freedom of a living, creative, cherishing thought and love. Throughout His life, the secret, utterly obedient conversation of Jesus with His Father goes on. He always snatches opportunities for it, and at every crisis He returns to it as the unique source of confidence and strength; the right and reasonable relation between the soul and its Source.

I thank thee, Heavenly Father, because thou hast hidden these things from the wise and prudent and revealed them unto babes. . . . Even so, Father, for so it seemed good in thy sight. . . . . I have kept my Father's commandment and abide in his love. . . . Father, the hour is come. . . . O righteous Father! the world knew thee not, but I knew thee. . . . Father, if thou be willing, remove this cup from me. . . . Father, forgive them . . . into thy hands I commend my spirit.

Though our human experience of God cannot maintain itself on such a level as this, yet for us too as members of Christ these words have significance. They set the standard of realism, of childlike and confident trust which must govern our relation to the Unseen. Abba, Father. The personalist note, never absent from a fully operative religion, is struck at the start; and all else that is declared or asked is brought within the aura of this relationship. Our sins, aims, struggles, sufferings, our easy capitulation to hopelessness and fear, look different over against that truth. Our responsibilities become simplified, and are seen to be one single, filial responsibility to God. Our Father, which art in heaven, yet present here and now in and with our struggling lives; on whom we depend utterly, as children of the Eternal Perfect whose nature and whose name is Love.

"Ye are of God, little children." Were this our realistic belief and the constant attitude of our spirits, our whole life, inward and outward, would be transformed. For we are addressing One who is already there, already in charge of the situation, and knowing far more about that situation than we do ourselves. Within His span it already lies complete, from its origin to its end: "Your Father knoweth what things ye have need of before you ask him." The prevenience of God is the dominant fact of all life; and therefore of the life of prayer. We, hard and loveless, already stand in heaven. We open the stiff doors of our hearts and direct our fluctuating wills to a completely present Love and Will directing, molding, and creating us. One aspect of redemption and one meaning of the incarnate life of Christ is to show men how to love this Present God, who comes to us in this thing and that thing, yet who induces in us a thirst and a longing that cannot be satisfied by any other thing than Himself alone.

And moreover in these first words, the praying soul accepts once for all its true status as a member of the whole family of man. Our Father. It can never again enter into prayer as a ring-fenced individual, intent on a private relation with God; for this is a violation of the law of Charity. Its prayer must overflow the boundaries of selfhood to include the life, the needs of the race; accepting as a corollary of its filial relation with God a brotherly relation with all other souls however diverse, and at every point replacing "mine" by "ours." This wide spreading love, this refusal of private advantage is the very condition of Christian prayer; for that prayer is an instrument of redemptive action, not merely of personal achievement. It is true that there is a bracing solitude of the spirit in which is realized the secret and unique relationship of each soul with God; for each its own place, its own prayer. But these personal responses and experiences, sacred and unrepeatable, take place within that one great movement of man's prayer of which the Church's corporate worship is the sacrament. Here my enemy prays by my side, since the world of prayer has no frontiers; and in so doing he ceases to be my enemy, because we meet in God.

When to this classic model we add those other teachings on prayer in which Christ recommends great hiddenness as toward men, and great humility, initiative, persevering faith, as toward God, we get the picture of a secret but most actual supernatural activity, detached from the distractions of earth and set toward another center of desire. This secret life is to be prosecuted with courage, confidence, and zest: asking, seeking, and knocking with the assurance of the child, not with the desperation of the lost and starving slave. The soul that says "Abba" cannot conceive of God as One who treats us worse than we treat the children whom we love. "All is ours." It is for us to throw down the barriers, quench the flame of separation, accept the unspeakable gift, find the hidden and awaiting treasure, and go forward to the frontier of unspeakable experiences, which fulfill and more than fulfill the utmost cravings of the soul, yet are part of the neglected heritage of man. Then, appeals for rescue and protection, requests for the alleviation of this or that earthly difficulty or pain are perceived to be beside the point: for these pains and difficulties will be the actual occasion of gratitude, once they are seen in spiritual regard as instruments of the perfecting of the soul. Our Father. We appeal by allusion to a character of Reality which is itself mysterious, yet which we can discern, because it is faintly reflected in our human experience. Beyond lies the unknown, the unreflected mystery of the Godhead. Between this homeliness and that transcendence there is no stopping place for the soul. Yet, because there can be no conflict in the simplicity of the Divine Nature, we know that within it these extremes are united. The ulti-

mate mystery is favorable to us; and our truest relation is that of filial trust.

"The Father is our Fount and Origin, in whom
our life and being is begun."[8] If this is our true situation, our relation to supreme Reality, that truth must
rule our lives. Whether considered in philosophic or
devotional regard, the thought is overwhelming. It
rebukes the anthropocentric bias of our theologians,
and the petty sentimentalisms of our self-centered
piety. We are the children not of earth but of heaven;
inheritors of a supernatural world of independent
beauty, unaffected by our nursery achievements and
untarnished by our nursery sins. Interrogating our
deepest nature, we discover in ourselves, as Ruysbroeck says, the Unconfined. In spite of the twist
which sin has given to us as a part of the created
order, the hard-set deformation of the soul, the
violence and cruelties of the life in which we are
immersed, our essential kinship with Holiness
remains. "The Father," said St. Paul to his fellow
Christians, "has made us fit to share the inheritance
of the Saints in light."[9]

God, who stands so decisively over against our
life, the Source of all splendor and all joy, is yet in
closest and most cherishing contact with us; and
draws us, beyond all splendor and all joy, into Truth.
He has created in us such a craving for Himself

---

8. [Jan Van] Ruysbroeck, *Adornment of the Spiritual Marriage*,
Bk. III, cap 3.

9. Col. 1, 12.

alone, that even the brief flashes of Eternity which sometimes visit us make all else seem dust and ashes, lifeless and unreal. Hence there should be no situation in our life, no attitude, no preoccupation or relationship, from which we cannot look up to this God of absolute Truth and say, "Our Father" of ourselves and of all other souls involved. Our inheritance *is* God, our Father and Home. We recognize Him, says St. John of the Cross, because we already carry in our hearts a rough sketch of the beloved countenance. Looking into those deeps, as into a quiet pool in the dark forest, we there find looking back at us the Face we implicitly long for and already know.[10] It is set in another world, another light: yet it is here. As we realize this, our prayer widens until it embraces the extremes of awestruck adoration and confident love and fuses them in one.

10. *The Spiritual Canticle,* 2nd Version, stanza xii.

Chapter III

THE NAME

Hallowed be Thy Name. The modern mind, living sometimes prudently and sometimes carelessly, but never theocentrically, cannot make anything of such words as these; for they sweep the soul up, past the successive and the phenomenal, and leave it in abject adoration before the single reality of God. They mean in all experiences, undertakings, and situations, a perpetual reference to that reality as the fact governing all judgments and all activities. This, says our Lord in effect, is the way that you must begin, because this is the essence of religion. For this, and only for this, it exists. When He is asked for the secret of prayer, "the true tent of meeting which the Lord pitched and not man,"[11] this delighted recognition of God's priority comes first to His mind. Let everything that hath breath praise the Lord! This is what creation is for: and the very object of man's transformation is that he may become part of this inner life of the universe, which consists in the praise, the glory, the manifestation of God. St. John of the Cross says that creation babbles to us, like a child which cannot articulate what it wants to say;

---

11. Heb. 8, 2.

for it is struggling to utter the one Word, the Name and character of God.[12]

Since for Christians the Nature and the Name of God is Love, this means a deep reverence for love in all its manifestations: on one hand as the power which holds the Universe together, on the other as the unearthly glory, the Shekinah, which in every situation declares the presence of the Holy and transfigures earthly life. Love is always to be recognized and adored, for it is the signature of God lying upon creation; often smudged and faded, almost blotted out, yet legible to the eyes which have been cleansed by prayer. It is the peculiar wisdom of the saints that they can read the letters of the Name wherever found and in whatever script; as Francis read them on the face of the Crucified, in the marred features of the leper, and written in the air by the moving wings of the free birds. These hear the utterance of the Name in all the voices of creation, gruff and gentle, the mating cry of lions and the call of the plover to her straying children; for the saints are realists, centered on God, and understand all life at every level in terms of worship. "All created things," says [Jean-Pierre] de Caussade, "are living in the Hand of God. The senses see only the action of the creature; but faith sees in everything the action of God."[13] Eros no less than Agape proceeds from Him; the stammer-

---

12. Op. cit., stanza vii.

13. *L'Abandon à la Providence Divine*, Cap. II, 1.

ing utterance, in a world otherwise perverse and violent, of the Name which even angels cannot pronounce aright.

Thus, Christ places at the opening of the life of prayer an aspiration which sums up the desire of the whole created order: an aspiration too great for the mind and therefore great enough for the soul, proclaiming at once the priority and mysterious call of the Supernatural, and the true vocation of Man. Indeed, the very reason for the Church's existence is the more perfect hallowing of the Name; for the Church is the Body in and through which the Son, the Logos, utters the praise of the Father. Men are redeemed out of slavery to time into the freedom of eternal life, that they may take their small part in this eternal act of sacrificial worship.

Before the glorious seat of thy Majesty, O Lord, and the exalted throne of thine honor and the awful judgment seat of thy burning love and the absolving altar which thy command hath set up, and the place where thy glory dwelleth, we, thy people and the sheep of thy fold, do kneel with thousands of the cherubim singing alleluia, and many times ten thousand seraphim and archangels acclaiming thine holiness, worshipping, confessing and praising thee at all times, O Lord of all![14]

---

14. Chaldean Liturgy.

Here we are given the direct claim of Eternity on our devotion: embracing and transcending all other aspects of religion, and entincturing with reality all such other expressions of religion as our small spirits can contrive. Our Father . . . hallowed be Thy Name. With one hand we touch the most secret intimacies of the spirit, our loving and childlike relation to God, with the other the creature's unlimited awe before His mystery: a mystery which grows deeper, the nearer we approach. As the awe with which we look up at the mountain from the valley is nothing to the awe which fills us when we stand alone among the glaciers, so the development of our prayer must always bring with it a dim yet certain sense of the great reserves, the dread and secret life, of the Godhead over against us, which kills cheap and familiar sentimentalisms at birth.

"It is those who know most of God," says St. John of the Cross, "who understand most clearly the infinite reaches of His being which remain uncomprehended by us."[15] Here, as in every approach to Reality, to Holiness, to Beauty, it is those who see much, not those who see little, who realize how much remains unseen. That is why the theologian always has plenty to say about God; while the contemplative can hardly say anything at all. The fluent teacher, with his sharp outlines and his neat list of attributes, is only the man with the telescope, not the

---

15. *The Spiritual Canticle,* loc. cit.

Alpine guide. Real prayer must ever be an entering into ignorance, a timid upward gaze toward the splendor which baffles the mind while it satisfies the heart. The ceremonial acts of organized religion are dramatic representations of this bowing down of our fragmentary intelligences before the "intellectual radiance full of love." Thus worship, since it is always an encounter with perfection, brings with it a crisis, a judgment; conviction of sin, and the cause of conviction of sin. Here at once we are confronted by the austere element in the life of faith, the utter abasement of the creature before the Holy; and are reminded that Love is a grave and ruthless passion, unlimited in self-giving and unlimited in demand.

And next, this first response of creation to its author, this awestruck hallowing of the Name, must also be the first response of the praying soul. If we ask how this shall be done within the individual life and what it will require of us in oblation and adjustment, perhaps the answer will be something like this: "Our Father, which art in heaven, hallowed, revered, be Thy mysterious Name in my dim and fluctuating soul, to which Thou hast revealed Thyself in such a degree as I can endure. May all my contacts and relationships, my struggles and temptations, thoughts, dreams, and desires be colored by this loving reverence. Let me ever look through and beyond circumstance to Thee, so that all I am and do may become more and more worthy of the God who is the origin of all. Let me never take such words on my lips that I could not pass from them to the hallowing of Thy Name. (That one principle alone, consistently applied, would bring order and charity into the center of my life.) May that Name, too, be hallowed in my work, keeping me in remembrance that Thou art the doer of all that is really done: my part is that of a humble collaborator, giving of my best." This means that adoration, a delighted recognition of the life and action of God, subordinating everything to the Presence of the Holy, is the essential preparation for action. That stops all feverish strain, all rebellion and despondency, all sense of our own importance, all worry about our own success; and so gives dignity, detachment, tranquillity to our action and may make it of some use to Him.

Thus the four words of this petition can cover, criticize, and reinterpret the whole of our personal life; cleansing it from egoism, orienting it toward reality, and reminding us that our life and work are without significance, except insofar as they glorify that God to whom nothing is adequate though everything is dear. Our response to each experience which He puts in our path, from the greatest disclosure of beauty to the smallest appeal to love, from perfect happiness to utmost grief, will either hallow or not hallow His Name; and this is the only thing that matters about it. For every call to admiration or to sacrifice is an intimation of the Holy, the Other, and opens a path leading out from self to God. These words, then, form in themselves a complete prayer; an aspiration which includes every level and aspect of life. It is the sort of prayer that both feeds and expresses the life of a saint, in its absolute disinterestedness and delighted abasement before the Perfection of God.

From one point of view the rest of the Lord's Prayer is simply about the different ways in which this adoring response of creation can be made more complete; for its asks for the sanctification of the universe. And by universe we do not mean some vast abstraction. We mean everything that exists, visible and invisible; the small as well as the great, the hosts of earth as well as the hosts of heaven; the mouse's tail as well as the seraph's wing brought into the circle of holiness and transfigured by the radiance of God. All creatures without exception taking part in the one great utterance of the Name: all self-interested striving transformed into that one great striving for the Glory of God which is the whole life of heaven and should be the whole life of earth.

"If," says Martin Buber, "you explore the life of things and of conditioned being you come to the unfathomable, if you deny the life of things and of conditioned being, you stand for nothingness, if you hallow this life you meet the living God."[16] Here is declared that principle of cosmic order which must govern the coming of the Kingdom and doing of the Will; and shall at its term convert the whole world of action into an act of worship. Since this world of action includes the small but powerful movements of the individual soul, here too the law of the Cosmos is to be applied. For this soul's life, if indeed that

---

16. *Ich und Du,* ["I and Thou"], Pt. III.

soul is truly living, must be that of a spirit standing in adoration before the Lord and Giver of its life; and its response to its surroundings physical and spiritual, in love and pain, fulfillment and sacrifice, in home, work, social contacts, aesthetic and intellectual experience must subserve this, its first duty. All must be brought to the altar and consecrated to the purposes of the Holy. All, directly or overtly, must hallow the Name of God.

If the transforming power of religion is to be felt, its discipline must be accepted, its price paid in every department of life; and it is only when the soul is awakened to the reality and call of God, known at every point of its multiple experience, that it is willing to pay the price and accept the discipline. Worship is a primary means of this awakening.

It follows once more that wholehearted adoration is the only real preparation for right action: action which develops within the Divine atmosphere, and is in harmony with the eternal purposes of God. The Bible is full of illustrations of this truth, from the call of Isaiah to the Annunciation. First the awestruck recognition of God: and then, the doing of His Will. We cannot discern His Eternal Purpose, even as it affects our tiny lives, opportunities, and choices, except with the eyes of disinterested and worshiping love. The hallowing of the Name is therefore the essential condition without which it is not possible to work for the Kingdom or recognize the pressure of the Will. So the first imperative of the life of prayer is that which the humanist finds so hard to understand. We are to turn our backs upon earth, and learn how to deal with its sins and its needs by looking steadfastly up to heaven.

Yet the life of prayer is incomplete if it stops here, in the realm of aspiration. Costly action as well as delighted fervor must form part of it. Like all else in the spiritual life of animal man, it must have its sacramental expression. Heroic sacrifice, peaceful suffering, patient and inconspicuous devotion to uncongenial tasks, the steady fight against sin, ugliness, squalor, and disease, the cleansing of national thought and increase of brotherhood among men: all this is a true part of the hallowing of the Name. It is our response to the impact of Perfection, our active recognition of the claim of God. Awe alone is sterile. But when it is married to sacrificial love, the fruits of the Spirit begin to appear; and the hallowing of the Name and the working for the Kingdom are seen to be two sides of one reality—the response of the creature to the demand of Love.

For Christians, there can be no limit to this consecration of life; in all things and at all costs putting the Holy first. The royal law must govern, even in those situations dark to faith when the demand of God, the call to sacrifice, cuts right across the texture of life and seems to oppose prudence and common sense. Here our modern humanitarianisms and sentimentalisms, our ceaseless attempts to harness the supernatural in the interests of our dark Satanic mills, look very cheap and thin over against the solemn realities of religion, the awful priority of God, which the Bible forces again and again on our reluctant and utilitarian minds. Abraham leading

Isaac up Mount Moriah is perhaps too hard a sacrament of worship for the modern Christian to digest. But the principle is summed up and driven home with less violence, yet with all the weight that history can give, in the story of King David and Ornan the Jebusite.[17]

David is told by his seer that he must build an altar to God on Ornan's threshing floor. To a mind bent on man and his legitimate interests, the suggestion is outrageous. All social and economic considerations are against it: for the threshing floor is a necessity of Ornan's livelihood. When the demand comes, he is threshing wheat on it, performing one of the essential duties of his practical farming life. King David, with the hesitation of a prudent monarch forced to make an unpopular demand, asks for the threshing floor and offers an adequate price. And suddenly the simple farmer, in his passionate generosity, his vivid sense of the overruling demand of God, towers over the careful piety of the King; so anxious that religion shall not cause any trouble with the people. Ornan is not even content to give what is asked, though this already strikes at a central need of his life. He knows that his only possible answer is total, delighted sacrifice. "And Ornan said, Take it to thee . . . lo! I give thee the oxen for burnt offerings and the threshing instruments for wood, and the wheat for the meal offering. I give it all!"—the final vow, the total consecration, the unconditioned sur-

---

17. I Chron. 21, 18.

render to God. Everything offered in oblation without stopping to count the cost. Hallowed be Thy Name.

Out of the mists of Jewish history, with its savage cruelties, its primitive and uneven reactions to the dawning light of the divine, comes this perfect picture of a flawless response to God's demand. All the Jebusite farmer's useful and necessary work, his human achievement and his future needs are offered, the very tools of his craft turned into fuel, the wheat for the coming winter sacrified. I give it all, that so this place may be holy to the Lord. Thus the site of Solomon's Temple was sanctified; and a place was prepared for the Holy of Holies, the Ark and the Mercy Seat. Those who stand today in the temple area of Jerusalem, stand on the threshing floor which was offered without condition by Ornan the Jebusite. There Isaiah saw the Seraphim; there the child Jesus, near the end of its long history, was presented before God; there He watched the widow give her mite; then He cast out those who dared to mingle man's profit with God's praise. An unbroken chain leads from the farmer's offering to the Cross.

Chapter IV
THE KINGDOM

Having recognized and worshiped the Name, we pray next for its triumph: Thy Kingdom come. Here man's most sacred birthright, his deep longing for perfection, and with it his bitter consciousness of imperfection, break out with power. We want to bring the God whom we worship, His beauty, His sovereignty, His order, into the very texture of our life; and the fundamental human need for action into the radius of our prayer. This is the natural sequel to the prayer of adoration. We have had a glimpse of the mystery of the Holy, have worshiped before the veils of beauty and sacrifice; and that throws into vivid relief the poverty, the anarchy, the unreality in which we live—the resistance of the world, the creature, to God, and its awful need of God.

Thy Kingdom come! We open our gates to the Perfect, and entreat its transfiguring presence; redeeming our poor contingencies, our disharmonies, making good our perpetual fallings short. We face the awful contrast between the Actual and the Real, and acknowledge our need of deliverance from sin; especially that sin of the world, that rebellion of creation against the Holy, which has thrust us out of heaven. The Kingdom is the serenity of God already enfolding us, and seeking to penetrate and redeem the whole of this created order; "shattering the horror of perpetual night" by a ray of heavenly brightness. We pray for this transformation of life, this healing of its misery and violence, its confusion and unrest, through the coming of the Holy God whom we adore; carrying through to regions still unconquered the great, the primary petition for the hallowing of His Name. That the Splendor over against us may enter, cleanse, and sanctify every level of our existence; give it a new quality, coherence, and meaning.

The prayer is not that we may come into the Kingdom, for this we cannot do in our own strength. It is that the Kingdom, the Wholly Other, may come to us, and become operative within our order; one thing working in another, as leaven in our dough, as seed in our field. We are not encouraged to hope that the social order will go on evolving from within, until at last altruism triumphs and greed is dethroned: nor indeed does history support this view. So far is this amiable program from the desperate realities of our situation, so unlikely is it that human nature will ever do the work of grace, that now we entreat the Divine Power to enter history by His Spirit and by His saints; to redeem, cleanse, fertilize, and rule. Nor is this tremendous desire, this direct appeal to the Transcendent, that of one or two ardent and illuminated souls: it is to be the constant prayer of the whole Church, voicing the one need of the whole world. "We know that the whole creation groaneth and travaileth in pain together until now. And not only so, but ourselves also, which have the first fruits of the Spirit."[18]

The world is not saved by evolution, but by incarnation. The more deeply we enter into prayer the more certain we become of this. Nothing can redeem the lower and bring it back to health, but a life-giving incursion from the higher; a manifestation of the already present Reality. "I came forth from the Father, and am come into the world": and this perpetual advent—the response of the eternal Agape to Eros in his need—is the true coming into time of the Kingdom of Heaven. The Pentecostal energy and splendor is present to glorify every living thing: and sometimes our love reaches the level at which it sees this as a present fact, and the actual is transfigured by the real.

What we look for then is not Utopia, but something which is given from beyond: Emmanuel, God with us, the whole creation won from rebellion and consecrated to the creative purposes of Christ. This means something far more drastic than the triumph of international justice and good social conditions. It means the transfiguration of the natural order by the supernatural: by the Eternal Charity. Though we achieve social justice, liberty, peace itself, though we give our bodies to be burned for these admirable causes, if we lack this we are nothing. For the Kingdom is the Holy not the moral; the Beautiful not the

---

18. Rom. 8, 22, 23.

correct; the Perfect not the adequate; Charity not law.

With our growth in the spiritual life, we gradually learn this lesson of the complete difference in kind between our kingdom, our aim and achievement even at its best, and the Kingdom and achievement of God: that even the most devoted efforts for the moral and spiritual improvement of the here and now stop short of the real need—that total redemption of a distorted world for which "the earnest expectation of the creature waiteth"; its reharmonizing with reality. The rule of Charity, which is the same as the sovereignty of the Holy, can never be forced on a reluctant world; for this is not consistent with its nature. God will not invade His lost province. His Spirit conquers by penetration, entering by the open door of prayer and spreading to entincture the whole of life. "Our God shall come and shall not keep silence"; but the coming will be very quiet. Without observation, the Eternal slides into the successive by inconspicuous paths, and transforms it to its purpose; the humble birth in a crowded stable yard outside Jerusalem, the victory of love when a young prophet gave himself to the Father's purpose on the Cross, when a young scholar capitulated to that same Cross on the road to Damascus, when a young poet kissed a leper outside the gates of Assisi. And many times more when homely heroisms, quiet sacrifices, secret prayers have opened the door. For the action of God is seldom showy; the true energies of the Kingdom are supersensuous— only a little filters through to the visible world.

Thus more and more we must expect our small action to be overruled and swallowed up in the vast Divine action; and be ready to offer it, whatever it may be, for the fulfillment of God's purpose, however much this may differ from our purpose. The Christian turns again and again from that bewildered contemplation of history in which God is so easily lost, to the prayer of filial trust in which He is always found; knowing here that those very things which seem to turn to man's disadvantage, may yet work to the Divine advantage. On the frontier between prayer and history stands the Cross, a perpetual reminder of the price by which the Kingdom is brought in. Seen from the world's side, it is foolishness; seen from the land of contemplation, it is the Wisdom of God. We live in illusion till that wisdom has touched us; and this touch is the first coming of the Kingdom to the individual soul.

It is a great thing for any soul to say without reserve in respect of its own life, "Thy Kingdom come!" for this means not only the acknowledgment of our present alienation, our fundamental egoism and impurity, but the casting down of the will, the destruction of our small natural sovereignty; the risk and adventure which accompany an unconditional submission to God, a total acceptance of the rule of love. None can guess beforehand with what anguish, what tearing of old hard tissues and habits, the Kingdom will force a path into the soul, and confront self-love in its last fortress with the penetrating demand of God. Yet we cannot use the words, unless we are prepared to pay this price: nor is the prayer of adoration real, unless it leads on to this. When we said, "Hallowed be Thy Name!" we acknowledged the priority of Holiness. Now we offer ourselves for the purposes of Holiness: handing ourselves over to God that His purposes, great or small, declared or secret, natural or spiritual, may be fulfilled through us and in us, and all that is hostile to His Kingdom done away.

There will be two sides to this: passive and active. The passive side means enduring, indeed welcoming, the inexorable pressure of God's transforming power in our own lives; for the Kingdom comes upon earth bit by bit, as first one soul and then another is subjugated by love and so redeemed. It means enduring the burning glance of the Holy, where that glance falls on imperfection, hardness, sin. The active side means a self-offering for the purposes of the Kingdom, here and now in this visible world of space and time; the whole drive of our life, all our natural endowments, set toward a furtherance of the purposes of God. Those purposes will not be fulfilled till the twist has been taken out of experience, and everything on earth conforms to the pattern in heaven—that is to say, in the Mind of God: wide-spreading love transfiguring the whole texture of life. Here we have a direct responsibility as regards our whole use of created things: money, time, position, the politics we support, the papers we read. It is true that the most drastic social reform, the most complete dethronement of privilege, cannot of themselves bring the Kingdom in; for peace and joy in the Holy Spirit can only come to us by the free gift of the Transcendent. But at least these can clear the ground, prepare the highway of God; and here each act of love, each sacrifice, each conquest of prejudice, each generous impulse carried through into action counts: and each unloving gesture, hard judgment, pessimistic thought or utterance opposes the coming of the Kingdom and falsifies the life of prayer.

The coming of the Kingdom is perpetual. Again and again freshness, novelty, power from beyond the world, break in by unexpected paths, bringing unexpected change. Those who cling to tradition and fear all novelty in God's relation with His world deny the creative activity of the Holy Spirit, and forget that what is now tradition was once innovation: that the real Christian is always a revolutionary, belongs to a new race, and has been given a new name and a new song. God is with the future. The supernatural virtue of hope blesses and supports every experiment made for the glory of His Name and the good of souls: and even when violence and horror seem about to overwhelm us, discerns the secret movement of the Spirit inciting to sacrifice and preparing new triumphs for the Will. In the Church too this process of renovation from within, this fresh invasion of Reality, must constantly be repeated if she is to escape the ever-present danger of stagnation. She is not a static institution, but the living Body of the living Christ—the nucleus of the Kingdom in this world. Thus loyalty to her supernatural calling will mean flexibility to its pressures and demands, and also a constant adjustment to that changing world to which she brings the unchanging gifts. But only insofar as her life is based on prayer and self-offering will she distinguish rightly between these implicits of her vocation and the suggestions of impatience or self-will.

Yet the coming of the Kingdom does not necessarily mean the triumph of this visible Church; nor of that which is sometimes called the Christian social order. It means something far more deep, subtle, and costly: the reign of God, the all-demanding and all-loving, in individual hearts, overruling all the "adverse powers" which dominate human life— the vigorous survivals from our animal past which are nourished by our egotism and support its implicit rebellion against God—fear and anger, greed and self-assertion, jealousy, impatience and discontent. It means the reordering, the quieting, the perfecting of our turbulent interior life, the conquest of our rampant individualism by God's supernatural action; and that same supernatural action gradually making each human life what it is meant to be—a living part of the Body of Christ, a sacramental disclosure of the splendor of God.

This secret and unrepeatable relation of each soul with God in prayer is the true condition of the well-being of the Church; for it is through these individual and derivative spirits that Holy and Absolute Spirit works in time. If the individual Christian depends on the support of the Supernatural Society, no less does that Supernatural Society depend on the quality of the individual Christian; and this quality is conditioned by his prayer—that is, the faithfulness, humility, and self-oblivion with which he responds to the pressure of God and offers himself for the purposes of the Will.

To look with real desire for the coming of the Kingdom means crossing over to God's side; dedicating our powers, whatever they may be, to the triumph of His purpose. The Bible is full of a stern insistence on that action which is ever the corollary of true contemplation. It is here that the praying spirit accepts its most sacred privilege: active and costly cooperation with God—first in respect of its own purification, and then in respect of His creative and redeeming action upon life. Our attitude here must be wide open toward God, exhibiting quite simply our poverty and impurity, acknowledging our second-rateness, but still offering ourselves such as we are. Thy Kingdom come! Here am I, send me. Not the nature lover's admiration but the laborer's hard work turns the cornfield into the harvest field. Hard work, which soon loses the aura of romantic devotion and must be continued through drudgery and exhaustion to the end.

When we realize this, and volunteer for it, at once we have about us the tremendous energies of the Saints; the great cooperators with the Holy, the delighted slaves of God at their infinitely varied tasks—yet all in one way or another proclaiming the imminent Kingdom, bringing the Eternal Charity into immediate contact with the creature's imperfections and needs. If we consider Christ's own action, as he moves, a man among men, declaring the Kingdom of God, we see that He sets about this in the most practical way: not merely inviting men to think of the Transcendent, but bringing down into the texture of their lives the redeeming action of the Transcendent. He is singularly uninterested in lofty ideas and large projects, but greatly interested in redemptive acts. "Jesus," says St. Matthew, "went about in all Galilee, preaching the good news of the Kingdom and healing all manner of disease and all manner of sickness among the people." He was acting as the link between the outpouring love and harmony of the Life of God, and the jangled and defective life of men. "Tell John the blind see, the lame walk, the lepers are cleansed." Human life is readjusted and made whole by the healing action of dynamic love, exercised by One whose life is identical with His prayer. His injunctions to His agents follow the same lines. They are to heal disharmony and misery wherever they find it, meeting with an eager and compassionate love the most repulsive aspects of life, touching the leper, ministering to the neurotic, seeking the degraded and the lost.

Christ announced the one and only purpose of His ministry to be the bringing in of the Kingdom of God; by the quiet action of a flawless love giving back to our lost tormented planet its place in the orchestra of heaven. Yet the way in which He spoke of this Kingdom, this victory of the Supernatural, was always allusive, suggestive, poetic—never precise. The Mystery of the Kingdom is sacred and must be reverenced. Again and again we are warned against any attempt to reduce it to a formula, to say, "Lo here! lo there!" to be dogmatic. Instead of definition we are given a series of vivid contrasting pictures of some of the things that it is like: oblique approaches to a single living Truth. Its inconspicuousness from our point of view and yet its tremendous latent energy—like seed which has in itself the whole life of the tree: like leaven working unseen the transformation of the dough. Its overwhelming attraction for those who recognize it—the Pearl, the Treasure. The Saints selling all they have to buy that Pearl, abandoning everything for the field in which the Treasure is hidden: prudence obliterated by love. In telling of the Kingdom, He begins with the homely facts of daily life, but ends upon the summit of romance. The Pearl is like the Grail: something always here, but never actualized save in the experience of certain happy and single-minded souls. Useless to hunt for it. We light upon it suddenly, in its matchless and reticent beauty: then, all hinges upon whether we will sell everything and pay the price.

Again, the Kingdom is present already, mingling disguised with the untransformed and common life; and sometimes the form in which it meets us has no beauty that we should desire it. Then it must be recognized not by its looks but by its fruits. It enters the world that we know, as it were by the action of One who sows broadcast something which is not of the world we know—the good seed of Holiness, the supernatural life. Sows it, not in a nicely prepared corner, but in the open field, exposed to all weathers and all risks. There God's wheat and the devil's darnel, which looks at first glance just like wheat, grow together. Real charity and sham charity; the real

Christian and the self-occupied devotee. The hurried enthusiast, the keen reformer, eager to apply absolute standards, wants to pull up the darnel and leave the wheat. But the wise tolerance of God leaves both growing together, content that the genuine crop should be known by its yield.

Chapter V
THE WILL

The graph of Christian prayer conforms very closely to the central action of the Eucharist. First the Sanctus, the type of all adoring worship "with angels and archangels glorifying the Holy Name" and lifting heart and mind to the contemplation of Reality. Then the bread and wine, the ordinary stuff of life raised to the plane of sacrifice and freely offered that it may be blessed and transformed by the action of the Holy, made the food and salvation of the soul. And now we stand at the central point on which all this is poised: where the heavenly prayer and the earthly prayer meet. Our Father, which art in heaven . . . Thy Will be done on earth as it is in heaven. The Will: that mysterious attribute of the Living Godhead of which a little crumb is given to men, in order that it may be united in love to the Whole from which it came. Once again the priority of the Holy, the overruling interests of the Transcendent are reaffirmed as the very substance of the creature's adoring prayer.

With this prayer for the Will to be done on earth as in heaven, the soul is brought to a more complete self-opening and a new and personal cooperation with God: and with this to a new and creaturely conviction of its own helplessness, its fundamental need. For only the Logos, the express image of His Person, can do in perfection the Father's Will. So here, we pray for union with His indwelling spirit. *Anima Christi sanctifica me!*[19] Accept and transform my small energy of desire that it may become part of Thy great energy of desire. Only thus can I achieve the end for which I was made, and make my tiny contribution to the redemption of the world.

Fiat voluntas tua.[20] We cannot miss the dynamic note, the drive, indeed the passion in these words. They should be remembered by those who tell us, with a particularly unfortunate resort to the dangers of arbitrary choice, that our business as immortal spirits is to Be rather than Do. For in fact our very being involves us in activity. We are placed in succession, and within succession must actualize our deep instinct for the Real; must exercise the will, and use our responsibility of choice. We cannot call a halt. On the one hand we hold fast to the Abiding; on the other, we are required to do the Will in and through serial acts. A tension, a duality, is inevitable for us; we are the unstable, striving agents of a quiet unchanging Love. Thus only the Christian synthesis of Grace and Nature, Faith and Works, the working of the eternal within the transitory, meets the situation which is envisaged in this prayer for the unhindered accomplishment of the purposes of God. The true focus of desire for all deeply loving souls

---

19. "Soul of Christ, sanctify me."

20. "Thy will be done."

must be this triumph of the Will by the self-surrender and arduous perfecting, the deliberate sacrificial deeds of the creature in response to the Light sent forth and the Grace given.

We have come down in the course of our prayer from the Infinite to the Finite, from the splendor of God, His present yet unseizable loveliness, to our distracted world; which is meant to be part of that splendor, to radiate that loveliness. Here is the scene in which His will to perfection must be worked out through us, by us, in spite of us. "Thy will be done in earth, as it is in heaven." We do not know what possibilities, what mysteries, may still be hidden in the unexpressed design. Yet because each step of this descending prayer is a movement of faith, obedience, and love, we bring the Infinite with us; as did Christ Himself when He came down from His nights of communion on the mountain to His redemptive work among men. Here, again, the life of prayer follows the path of the Incarnation. The Wisdom that came forth from the mouth of the Most High entered deeply into the common life, and there accomplished His transforming and redeeming work. We too are not to experience eternity and take up our obligations in respect of it in some exalted other-worldly region; but here and now, right down in that common life which is also dear to God, finding in our homely experience the raw material of sacrifice, turning its humble duties and relationships into prayer. Be it unto me according to Thy Word—here, where I am. Not my will but Thine be done. This is the act of oblation which puts life without condition at God's disposal, and so transforms and sacramentalizes our experience, and brings the Kingdom in.

Here we arrive at a prayer of pure realism, which is also the prayer of confident love: for what the Will may be, and what it may entail for us, we do not know. The enthusiastic forward look toward the coming of the Kingdom, the triumph of the Perfect, is easy; less easy, the acceptance of those conditions through and in which it must enter and dominate the lives of men. But if adoration has indeed done its disentangling work, no hesitations will mar this simple movement of abandonment. Thy Will: I accept the rule of God, whatever it may be, for myself, as well as working for it—the prayer of docility. That means a total capitulation to the mysterious Divine purpose; war declared on individual and corporate self-centeredness, death to an earthbound, meticulous, or utilitarian piety. It asks of the soul a heroic and liberating dedication to the interests of Reality; that, transcending the problems and needs of our successive existence, we may be made partners in the one august enterprise of the Spirit. This, says St. Paul, is the very meaning of the Passion: "that they which live shall no longer live unto themselves ... wherefore, if any man is in Christ, he is a new creature"[21]—his interests have become identical with those of the supernatural world. "Our wills are ours to make them thine" is not a mere bit

---

21. 2 Cor. 5, 15, 17.

of Victorian moralizing, but an almost perfect description of man's metaphysical state. We ask for our own subordination to Reality, the neutralizing of the rebel will, the deep grace of abandonment. For only "in Christ" are the Absolute Will and the will of the creature plaited together, to make a single cord of love.

We all have a preconceived idea of the path which we are to follow, the way in which we shall use our talents best. But in the world of prayer, our eyes cleansed by adoration, we perceive and acknowledge that the initiative lies with God; and only with us insofar as we give our energy to Him and take up our inheritance as Children of God, recognizing and welcoming His quiet directive action, His steady pressure within life as the only thing that really matters about it. Nor is this recognition possible to any but those whose surrender is complete. "There is no more certain way of going wrong," says Grou, "than to take for the Will of God all which comes into our hearts or passes through our minds."[22] This means death to self-will however cunningly disguised; the work that we love done with zest and care, but done God's way not ours, at His pace not ours, for His glory not ours, and laid down without reluctance, as the movement of the Will demands. Also the drudgery that we do not love done too, because that is His will and not ours. Going into business with the single talent which we would prefer to keep

---

22. J. N. Grou, *Manuel des Âmes Intérieures. De l'Obéissance.*

clean and unsullied by the rough and tumble of life. Substituting the discipline of the workshop for the freelance activities of the gifted amateur. Taking on the job that needs doing, the machine that needs tending, and tending it in the right way, even though it gives little scope to our particular gifts; or accepting the situation quietly, when the job which we seemed to be doing rather well is taken away. "Thy Will be done" means always being ready for God's sudden No over against our eager and well-meaning Yes: His overruling of our well-considered plans for the increase of His Glory and advancement of His Kingdom, confronting us with His Cross—and usually an unimpressive Cross—at the least appropriate time. All self-willed choices and obstinacy, all feverish intensity drawn out of the work which we supposed to be work for Him; so that it becomes more and more His work in us. "The glorious Majesty of the Lord our God be upon us." Then our handiwork will prosper; not otherwise.

A strange reversal of fortune, the frustration of obviously excellent plans, lies behind most of the triumphs of Christian history. It was by an unlikely route that Christ Himself, the country carpenter, itinerant preacher, and victim of local politics, carried humanity up into God. It was in defiance alike of the probable and the suitable that St. Paul was chosen, seized, transmuted, and turned to the purposes of the Will. Stephen, full of grace and power, is snatched in the splendor of his faith to God; and His Will is achieved and the Catholic Church is created by the abrupt conversion of a brilliant young scholar to a small revivalist sect. If we think of St. Paul's situation at the opening of his apostolic life—the humiliating eating of his own words, the long-lived suspicion and unpopularity, and his constancy through it all—it becomes clear that only the immense pressure of God's Will, overwhelming all natural reluctances and desires, can account for it. Nor did the rest of St. Paul's life, mostly spent in exhausting, dangerous, and often disappointing labors, contain much food for ambition or self-love. Christian history looks glorious in retrospect; but it is made up of constant hard choices and unattractive tasks, accepted under the pressure of the Will. "In the volume of the book it is written of me, that I should fulfil Thy Will, O my God: I am content to do it."[23]

Sometimes this total dedication to the purposes of the Will means the vigorous, self-sacrificing work of the active life, carried up to heroic levels. Sometimes it means that same life, which seemed so devoted and so effective, turned into the deep and beautiful surrender of the passive life. This is a transformation which the practical Christian finds very hard to understand. What is the good of it? God is the good of it. He is Pure Being as well as Pure Act, and therefore that apparently passive life, since it gives Him undisputed sway, unhindered passage, is in fact the most fully active life; for the action is that of God, and so has nothing in it with which to feed our

---

23. Ps. 40, 10.

self-esteem. When our fussy surface activity, our restless volition ceases, we realize beneath it the deep unceasing action of the mysterious Will, Master of the Tides, real doer of all that is done.

Sometimes the mortification of selfhood, the demand for acceptance, docility, and trust goes deeper and strikes at the center of the soul's action; its willed response in prayer to God. Then, all those practices and feelings which it had too easily identified with its spiritual life are swept away. It is left in a great emptiness and silence, there to learn the ultimate lessons of self-abandonment; the entire subordination of the creature's small action and choices to the vast Divine action and choices, and therefore a quiet acceptance of God's firm yet gentle pressures on the life He is molding to His Will. Thus only can it actualize within experience the truth which rules and clarifies the whole of human existence: the sublime and effortless action of the Eternal Life and Love supporting, penetrating, and overruling all individual striving and achievement.

"All that is done in us, around us and by us," says de Caussade,

> contains and conceals the action of God. There it is most truly and certainly present, but invisible; so that it always surprises us, and we only recognize its working when it is withdrawn. If we could pierce the veil, and were alert and attentive, God would show Himself to us without ceasing, and we should realize His action in all that happens to us. To

each thing we should say, *Dominus est.* It is the Lord. And we should find in every circumstance that we had received a gift from God. We should consider all creatures as feeble tools in the hands of an all-powerful craftsman, and should easily recognize that we lack nothing, and that God's continual care gives us at each moment that which is best for us.[24]

So, Thy Will be done, while it includes and sanctifies the life of eager cooperation, leads out beyond this to the more difficult and powerful life of active surrender and acceptance. "Crucifying the flesh with the desires thereof," says St. Paul; a drastic prescription for the redemption of human life. Crucifying, condemning, and executing, not sins alone but Sin; all those personal desires, ambitions, plans, preferences, and affections which make us separate, self-acting entities instead of living cells of the Body of Christ. Even the deepest desire of the creature, its profound hunger for God, is to be borne unsatisfied; until by His choice and movement, not ours, it is satisfied. An interior life conceived on these lines does not mean an easy peace, a consoling religion. It means the fullest, most unquestioning abandonment possible to the soul as the only path to union with God. This abandonment is learned first through those small tests and deprivations which provide, as it were, a preliminary gymnastic of the Spirit;

---

24. *L'Abandon à la Providence Divine,* Vol. I, p. 23.

increasing in difficulty with our growth and gradually producing that suppleness, that easy docility to
circumstance, which is a mark of the surrendered
soul. All our spiritual and intellectual action is
included in the material on which this exacting discipline must work: prayer, thought, movements of
love and hate, pity, resentment, patience, wrath.
Also darkness, interior suffering and temptation;
the tumult, pain, even rebellion which come from
the impact of God's Perfection on the imperfect
and unstable soul of man. Indeed, since there is for
man no tension and no problem when God's Will
and human preference happen to agree, and in fact
the drive and demand of the Will is then hardly
perceived by us, it follows that it is most often in
suffering, willed and accepted, that the real transcendence of egoism is accomplished. This does
not mean that suffering is in itself holy; but that,
being what we are, it nearly always accompanies
our full acceptance of the Holy and its tremendous
demands.

And the last Will is to be done "as in heaven";
peacefully, joyfully, perfectly, the response of a deep
and disciplined love. Here, in this pure and disinterested relation of spirit to Spirit, is the clue to life's
meaning "for to step into pure relation is not to
disregard everything, but to see everything in the
Thou, not to renounce the world but to establish it
on its true basis."[25] It is not in observing and accept-

_____

25. M. Buber, *Ich and Du,* III.

ing the drift of the Cosmos, but in replying to the strange Voice which speaks from within and beyond the Cosmos that we are to find our peace. *Fiat mihi secundum verbum tuum.*[26] Not "its mysterious laws" but "Thy mysterious Word."

"This," says Osuna,

> is the *fiat* of the Blessed Virgin, in which consists the highest perfection of love, whose end is to conform us entirely in all things, whether in prosperity or adversity, with all our heart to the Beloved. . . . So that we not only suffer patiently and with an entire conformity whatever happens, but we pray that what we did not wish for may be done, for love delights no less in what God does in opposition to its prayer, than in its accomplishment.[27]

This ultimate Christian temper of joyful abandonment to the hidden purpose of the Wholly Other perfects and establishes the theocentric orientation of the soul. It reflects back to a deep consciousness of the already existent Kingdom, "the mystery of the self-evident, nearer to me than my *I*";[28] for there is little in the texture of the successive order to evoke it. Indeed, at every point history offers the Cross for that soul's acceptance. The cruelty, violence, and

---

26. "Be it done unto me according to Thy Word."

27. F. Osuna, *The Third Spiritual Alphabet,* Treatise 16.

28. M. Buber, op. cit., loc. cit.

injustice of men win their apparent triumph; and only within and through that triumph loving acquiescence in the Will achieves, in the teeth of circumstance, a final victory. So too in the individual life, the line droops, creative energy is withdrawn to reemerge in those who come after; perhaps in a form which we cannot understand or admire. Yet none of this matters. No personal consideration counts, so long as the Will is done. Here egoism dies and the temper of heaven, loving disinterestedness, is born.

Thus the Christian, if he is to find room for the completing opposites of his illogical experience, is obliged on one hand to say, "Thy Will be done on, in, and through this world with which Thou art present; which is by declaration the object of thy care and the garment of thy praise. Here I accept in simplicity the mysterious drama of creation and destruction, and with that my own contribution to the great purpose which I cannot discern. And yet too, Thy Will be done by me at all costs here and now, over against this rebel world which so decisively rejects it." Christian life and prayer must accept this paradox, moving to and fro between abandonment and effort; for whatever we affirm in this sphere must at once be qualified by its opposite. "I have learned," said Nicholas of Cusa, "that the place wherein Thou art found unveiled is girt round with the coincidence of contradictories."[29]

---

29. *The Vision of God,* Cap. 9.

Chapter VI
FOOD

In the first part of the Lord's Prayer, we are wholly concerned with God's glory. We pray with angelic spirits; creatures whose purposes are completely harmonized with the Creative Will. In the second part, we turn from the Eternal Splendor to our earthly limitations, and bring before God the burden, neediness, and sinfulness of our state. Give us this day our daily bread. With this proclamation of our utter dependence, the presentation before God of the simplest and most fundamental of our needs, we pass from adoration to petition, and enter into the full paradox of Christian prayer: the unspeakable majesty and abiding perfection of the Infinite, and because of that majesty and that perfection, the importance of the claim of the fugitive, the imperfect, the finite.

The Heavens declare the Glory of God . . .
Lord, I call upon thee, haste thee unto me!

There is a natural tendency in man to reverse this order of approach; to come before God in a spirit of heaviness, greatly concerned with his own imperfections, needs, and desires—"my soul and its shortcomings," "the world and its wants"—and defer the putting on of the garment of praise: that wedding garment which introduces us into the company of the sons of God and is the only possible beginning of real prayer. Here, Christ's teaching and practice are decisive. First the heavenly, then the earthly. First ascend in heart and mind to the Eternal, adore the Father, seek the Kingdom, accept the Will: and all the rest shall be added unto you. Again and again the New Testament insists on that. The contrast of the two worlds is absolute; but their interpenetration is complete. No human need, however homely, is negligible; none lies outside the glow of God. There is no point however tiny on which the whole power of the Eternal Love does not play. Yet all the importance of the natural, the deep pathos of its need and imperfection, abides in its relation to God the Perfect and its dependence on Him; all its reality in the extent to which it expressses His Will. "Adam sinned when he fell from contemplation," because in that moment he lost the clue to the meaning of life. God is the First and the Last. We shall never grasp the meaning of our experience, see it in proportion, unless we begin by seeking His Face.

So now from the august vision of the supernatural order declaring His holiness, and the living Will which molds, supports, and penetrates His creation, "mightily and sweetly ordering all things," we turn, awed yet encouraged, to our little changing world; the homely arena within which the soul is required to glorify God. That changing world, too, is completely dependent on Him; incapable of embodying His will and beauty, unless fed, cleansed, and guided by the other-worldly Love. The second part of the Lord's Prayer, then, taking our situation as it is, brings before God the humbling realities of that natural life within which He finds us and calls us to the supernatural life, each in our own way and degree.

And first, our entire dependence. Give us this day our daily bread. In natural ways and in spiritual ways, man's successive spirit is maintained in constant and intimate dependence on the Eternal Spirit; and would fall into nothingness were that support withdrawn. Starvation both of body and soul is an ever-present possibility. "Thou feedest thy poor ones abundantly with heavenly loaves!" says an ancient prayer of the Spanish Church; a declaration beginning in man's Eucharistic experience, which spreads to embrace that primal Charity by which the cosmos is sustained. Indeed, this constant humbling dependence of the natural creature on food from beyond itself is a sacramental expression of a deeper mystery: the ceaseless self-imparting of God, the Food of the full-grown, to that childish soul which is being transformed into His image. Here our poetic symbols and our half-realized prayers move upon the surface of a Fact far too great for us—the substantial identity of Giver and Gift, God Himself as the soul's food. The prayer for our true Bread is a prayer for His self-imparting; and in the very prayer He is already given, for the petition of the creature and the self-imparting of the Creator are one moment.

"He is," says Jacopone da Todi,[30] "the *gran donatore,*
pastor and pasture of the soul." This secret prevenience of God, the all-sufficing Food and all-
cherishing Love, is the governing fact of the world
of prayer. Before Him, in Him, and by Him our
spirits live. His pressure on and in the soul and the
created world is ceaseless; coming by countless paths,
or rather with a total freedom which fills all channels, overflows all paths, and finds its opportunity in
every circumstance.

Nevertheless even here, where we know God's
self-giving to be absolute and our poverty to be complete, there is a certain demand upon our own effort.
Will must correspond with Grace. Man must use his
partial freedom, his power of choice, if he is indeed
to grow up and be capable of the Food of the full-
grown. God gives without stint all that the creature
needs, but it must do its part. He gives the wheat: we
must reap and grind and bake it. Even the Eucharistic gifts must cost us trouble, bear the imprint of
man's toil.

As, in the soul's life, will and grace rise and fall
together, so in its prayer effort and abandonment
are not alternatives, but completing opposites; and
without their rightful balance there is no spiritual
health. "If any will not work, neither shall he eat,"
said St. Paul; a precept of spiritual as well as practical application. "He gave them angels' food from
Heaven"; but they had to go out and gather the

---

30. Italian Franciscan poet and mystic, c. 1230–1306. (Eds.)

manna daily for themselves. The discipline of God is bracing; He gives the soul's food and gives it in abundance, but under conditions which make a wholesome demand on us. None are dispensed from taking trouble. And moreover the food is diverse according to the needs of each: "the way in which he is in tune with God, whether in outward good works or in the inward practice of love."[31] A sustaining and comforting meal for those called to the active life; hard crusts for interior souls. Here again, communion with God is never an experience imposed from without, but always a relation arising from within. On one hand, the humble and confident expectation, the upstretched neck and open beak of the hungry bird; on the other, the mysterious self-imparting of a steadfast and cherishing love: "For we feed upon His Immensity which we cannot devour, and we yearn after His Infinity which we cannot attain."[32]

Yet in dealing with the ways of God with man, the single image is never adequate to the facts. True, in the earlier stages of the life of prayer the soul is mainly conscious of a certain tension; of the object of desire, the satisfaction of hunger ever lying beyond its reach, the fullness of communion always missed, in spite of its own laborious humble effort. It is committed, as St. Teresa says, to hauling up the living water in its own bucket. The rope is harsh, the well

31. Ruysbroeck, *The Sparkling Stone,* Chap. 7.

32. Ruysbroeck, op. cit., Chap. 10.

is deep, and it never gets enough to quench its thirst. But presently it begins to realize that these hard and wholesome conditions do not impeach the free generosity of God. They are educational rather than inevitable, and exist chiefly for the soul's own sake; strengthening the will, developing the muscles, purifying the desire. Beyond and within all this is the steady, unfailing gift under many various disguises of Himself, the Living Water and the Living Food.

"Give us this day for bread the Word of God from Heaven," says a version of the Lord's Prayer found in the ancient Irish Gospels. Here man in his ignorance and fragility utters the one and all-sufficing prayer. For he is not fed by bread alone, not even by the appointed Bread of sacramental grace, but "by every word that proceeds from the Mouth of God"—all the utterances of the Spirit, all the messages given to him by and through life, and which make up life's significance. In all these, bitter or sweet, tasteless and dry or full of savor, God the Father of Spirits feeds our weak and childish spirits; that they may grow and ever more and more feed on Him. *Cresce et manducabis me.*

God gives Himself mainly along two channels: through the soul's daily life and circumstances and through its prayer. In both that soul must always be ready for Him; wide open to receive Him, and willing to accept and absorb without fastidiousness that which is given, however distasteful and unsuitable it may seem. For the Food of Eternal Life is mostly plain bread; and though it has indeed all sweetness and all savor for those who accept it with meekness and love, there is nothing in it to attract a more fanciful religious taste. All life's vicissitudes, each grief, trial, or sacrifice, each painful step in self-knowledge, every opportunity of love or renunciation, and every humiliating fall, have their place here. All give, in their various ways and disguises, the heavenly Food. A sturdy realism is the mark of this divine self-imparting, and the enabling grace of those who receive.

The offered Christ is distributed among us. Alleluia!
He gives his body as food and his blood he pours out for
* us. Alleluia!*
Draw near to the Lord and be filled with his light.
* Alleluia!*
Taste and see how sweet is the Lord. Alleluia![33]

The symbolism of food plays a large part in all religions, and especially in Christianity. As within the mysteries of the created order we must all take food and give food—more, must take life and give life—we are here already in touch with the "life-giving and terrible mysteries of Christ," who indwells that order; for all is the sacramental expression of His all-demanding and all-giving Life. We accept our constant dependence on physical food as a natural and inevitable thing. Yet it is not necessarily so: there are creatures which are free from it for long periods of time. But perhaps because of his bor-

33. Armenian Liturgy.

derline status, his embryonic capacity for God, man is kept in constant memory of his own fragility, unable to maintain his existence for long without food from beyond himself; his bodily life dependent on the humble plants and animals that surround him, his soul's life on the unfailing nourishment of the life of God. "I am the Bread of Life that came down from heaven. He that eateth of *this* bread shall live for ever." Eternal Life is the gift, the self-imparting of the Eternal God. We cannot claim it in our own right.

The Biblical writers make plain to us how easily and inevitably men have given spiritual rank to this primitive truth of life's dependence on food, and seen in it the image of a deeper truth which concerns the very ground of our being.

They give us the strange and haunting figure of Melchizedek, the King and Priest of Salem, of whom we are told so little yet feel we know so much. It is a picture which holds us by something which far transcends historic accuracy; something conveyed yet unexpressed, like the undertones of a great poem. While the other kings are fighting, slaying, disput-ing their spoils—living the full animal life of self-assertion and self-development—Melchizedek comes forth from his hilltop city, in a quiet majesty which we instinctively identify with holiness; bearing, not any signs of power, but bread and wine. He is the meek and royal minister of a generous God. This thought of the King and Priest, unarmed and unde-manding, bearing Bread and Wine from the Holy City to the poor fighters in the plain, cannot have

been far from our Lord's mind when, on the eve of
the turmoil and agony of the Passion, He blessed and
broke the loaves, took the chalice "into His holy and
venerable Hands" and gave thanks; and, with and
in this token sacrifice, gave Himself to be forevermore the food of men, "named of God a high priest
after the order of Melchizedek."[34] That noble movement of the ancient King, who did not await His
guests within the Holy City, but came forth as one
that serveth, bearing bread and wine, is indeed
a perfect image of the royal charity which comes
to seek men's souls on the plain where they struggle, bearing the gifts of eternal life. The Eastern
Churches have always called the Eucharistic elements the "gifts"; and in the ancient liturgies this
emphasis on an unspeakable free gift made to men
by God, "one heavenly Bread, one Food of the
whole world,"[35] is heard as a recurrent melody.

He gave them bread from heaven to eat.
Alleluia.
Having in itself all sweetness and all savor.
Alleluia.[36]

Throughout His ministry, our Lord emphasized
the idea of feeding as something intimately connected with His love and care for souls. The mystery

34. Heb. 5, 10.

35. Liturgy of St. James

36. Roman Breviary. Office for [the feast of] Corpus Christi.

of the Eucharist does not stand alone. It is the crest of a great wave; a total sacramental disclosure of the dealings of the Transcendent God with men. The hunger of man is the matter of Christ's first temptation. The feedings of the four thousand and the five thousand are more than miracles of practical compassion; we feel that in them something of deep significance is done, one of the mysteries of Eternal Life a little bit unveiled. So too in the Supper at Emmaus; when the bread is broken the Holy One is known. It is peculiar to Christianity, indeed part of the mystery of the Incarnation, that it constantly shows us this coming of God through and in homely and fugitive things and events; and puts the need and dependence of the creature at the very heart of prayer.

Chapter VII
FORGIVENESS

It is part of the economy of mercy, the redemptive and transforming work of God, that the Divine Charity already present within the soul should overflow to make good its shortcomings and blot out its sins. Were this not so, our situation would be hopeless; for we share by nature in the disorder of a fallen world, its implicit resistance to the demands of love. So here we continue our filial and confident claim on that Charity; a claim which our situation, whether as children or as creatures, compels us to make. Forgive us our trespasses—our voluntary share in the world's sinfulness—as we forgive them that trespass against us. Penitence is ever the fruit of adoring vision. "The more holy I find God," said [Baron Friedrich] von Hügel, "the more wicked I feel myself to be." "Thou the Holy, Thou the Strong." I, the unholy, feeble, sinful; yet able in my weakness to perceive Beauty and adore.

Once again the soul is brought to a closer, more personal apprehension of its true situation; is thrown yet more deeply into God. If we cannot live without His Life feeding and supporting us, still less can we live without His loving-kindness; tolerating our imperfections, rectifying our errors, forgiving our perpetual shortcomings and excesses, debts and trespasses, and giving us again and again another chance. His challenge stands over against us, in its eternal beauty and perfection: but we know that the standard of eternal perfection must not be applied to us. The adoring soul which worshiped with the seraphim and said, "Hallowed be Thy Name," now stands by the side of Isaiah and shares his creaturely shame. "Woe is me! For I am a man of unclean lips." We belong to an imperfect world. That downward pull, that declension from the light, which theology calls original sin, is felt at every level of our being. With the deepening of our experience we become more and more conscious of this. Hence the life of prayer is always a progress in lowliness; and now we arrive at the genuine and life-giving humility which is the fruit of seeing ourselves as we really are. "Glory be to thee! Have mercy upon me!" We take our lowly place, acknowledge our wretchedness; and on this poverty and helplessness we base our confident prayer for the indulgent gentleness of God.

Moreover, the scene in which we are placed makes its own drastic demand on prudence and courage. As de Tourville[37] says, it is useless for the Christian to look for a main road on which he can walk safely and steadily in his journey's end. Like the Swiss, he

---

37. Abbe Henri de Tourville (1842–1903), French priest and mentor of Underhill's own spiritual mentor, Friedrich von Hügel. (Eds.)

must learn that rough tracks are the native roads of his country; that we only become surefooted by long practice, and that slips and falls are sure to occur.[38] Sometimes we lose the path, sometimes trip over a stone, sometimes fall headlong in the mud. We are beset by invitations to stray; by the attractive short-cuts suggested by vanity, egoism, or fear. We stand in perpetual need of the kindness and patience of that God who is our Guide no less than our Goal, who picks us up, overlooks our frailties and follies, again and again puts us back on the path. "Forgive us our trespasses." A whole type of prayer, a special and intimate relation with the Unseen, brought into existence by the very fact of our mixed half-animal nature, the ceaseless tension between the pull of earth and the demand of heaven, is summed up in these four words.

The sequence of Antiphons which the ancient Church ordained for the opening days of Lent—a liturgical direction, as it were, for the intention of the penitent Christian soul—shows how many-sided is our creaturely need for the pitying indulgence and redeeming action of God. "Lord, that I may have light! . . . Wash me throughly from my wickedness, and cleanse me from my sin. . . . Lord, my servant lieth sick of the palsy. . . . Lord, I am not worthy that thou shouldst come under my roof: but say the word only and my soul shall be healed."

---

38. *Pensées Diverses*, p. 111.

Each phrase casts its searchlight on our condition. We need light, for the eyes of the mind are darkened, so that we cannot see the reality of our state; we need cleansing, for our very selfhood is sullied and impure. Our souls are sick and helpless, for sin has sapped their energy; we need a new dower of vitality from beyond ourselves if we are to become the sons of the Kingdom and serve the creative purpose of the Will. We end with an act of total and contrite confidence in God's restoring action—the crown of penitence: "Say the word only, and my soul shall be healed."

Over against the Glory of God, the Majesty of the Holy, the debtor, the penitent, the publican, the unsatisfactory and unharmonized creature who exists in each of us dares to claim his filial rights. Here stands one who constantly falls short and knows it; who is blinded by prejudice, sick of self-love, capable of hatred and envy, violence and fear; one who could have done more and did not, thought he was strong and turned out weak, should not have trespassed in pursuits of his own ends, and did: a child of God, not an outsider or an outcast, who now faces the facts and says, "Forgive!" Here, in the constant exercise of the divine economy of penitence and pardon, is one of the strongest links which binds the soul to God.

But this is not all. Were the mere escape from consequence, the blotting out of transgressions, the object of our prayer, how greatly it would fall beneath the level on which Christ has placed man's relation to God; and how easy a concession it would offer to our inveterate self-love. But instead of an easy concession, the divine forgiveness makes a heroic demand upon our courage. For that forgiveness is not the easy passing of a sponge over a slate. It is a stern and painful process; it means the reordering of the soul's disordered love, setting right what is wrong, washing it from wickedness and cleansing it from sin. Theology declares that original sin, disturbing the balance and harmony of man's nature, causes especially four kinds of spiritual damage: ignorance, malice, weakness, and claimful desire. Here are the roots of our worst deordinations; and these the Charity of God must cure. That Charity must compel self-knowledge, kill animosity, brace the will, and mortify desire. Playing without hindrance on the soul that craves for forgiveness it burns to heal; redeems, transforms, and purifies all at once. The Lord's Prayer contains no direct demand for purification because pardon, the restoration of a loving relation with the Perfect, involves purification. The penitent soul accepts the jurisdiction of Charity, and Charity will have its perfect and searching work: burning up the chaff in the unquenchable fire of love. The cleansing pains of contrition are part of the mercy of God.

That is one side, but only one side of the situation. What makes this position crucial is the power, the freedom of the sinner; the fact that he does not merely soil his own garments or lose his own way, but inflicts damage and suffering on his fellow creatures when he departs from the order of Charity. He has used his liberty for their destruction. He needs the forgiveness of men as well as the forgiveness of God. Through mere lack of loving imagination, through inveterate self-interest and self-protective hardness, or by deliberate intent, he has inflicted mental, emotional, and spiritual injury and added to the confusion and pain of the world. He is a culprit, a debtor. He has abused the sacred gift of freedom, and because of this things are worse than they were before. It is this desperate situation, whether corporate or individual, which we entreat God to accept and resolve: and this He can only do in one way— by making the utmost demand on the charity and humility of the creature, by a universal application of the law of generous love. Forgive us our trespasses, as we forgive them that trespass against us. We ask with confidence because we are the children of Love and have accepted its obligations, even though our own worst declensions will always be from Love itself, and our heaviest debts will be arrears of Charity. Yet here too, acknowledging our insufficiency, we are forgiven, if we try to look through the eyes of the divine pity on the failures of our brothers and sisters in love: forgetting our own injuries, however grievous, and remembering only our common tendency to sin.

There is no lesson Christ loves better to drive home, than this disconcerting fact of our common human fragility: which, when we have truly grasped it, kills resentment and puts indulgent pity in its place. Let the man, the group, the nation that is without sin cast the first stone. God's forgiveness means the compassionate recognition of that weakness and instability of man; how often we cannot help it, how truly there is in us a "root and ground of sin," an implicit rebellion against the Holy, a tendency away from love and peace. And this requires of us the constant compassionate recognition of our fellow creatures' instability and weakness; of the fact that they too cannot help it. If the Christian penitent dares to ask that his many departures from the Christian norm, his impatience, gloom, self-occupation, unloving prejudices, reckless tongue, feverish desires, with all the damage they have caused to Christ's Body, are indeed to be set aside, because—in spite of all—he longs for God and Eternal Life; then he too must set aside and forgive all that the impatience, selfishness, bitter and foolish speech, sudden yieldings to base impulse in others have caused him to endure. Hardness is the one impossible thing. Harshness to others in those who ask and need the mercy of God sets up a conflict at the very heart of personality and shuts the door upon grace. And that which is true of the individual soul, is also true of the community; the penitent nation seeking the path of life must also conform to the law of charity.

This principle applied in its fullness makes a demand on our generosity which only a purified and self-oblivious love can hope to meet. For every soul that appeals for God's forgiveness is required to move over to His side, and share the compassionate understanding, the unmeasured pity, with which He looks on human frailty and sin. So difficult is this to the proud and assertive creature, that it comes very near the end of our education in prayer. Indeed, the Christian doctrine of forgiveness is so drastic and so difficult, where there is a real and deep injury to forgive, that only those living in the Spirit, in union with the Cross, can dare to base their claim on it. It means not only asking to be admitted to the Kingdom of Redeeming Love, but also declaring our willingness to behave as citizens of that Kingdom even under the most difficult conditions; the patriot king forgiving the invaders of his country, the merciful knight forgiving his brother's murderer and sheathing his sword before the crucifix, the parent forgiving his daughter's betrayer, the devoted reformer forgiving those who have ruined his life's work, the lover of peace forgiving the maker of war. Cruelty, malice, deceit, and violence doing their worst; and seen by us through the eyes of a pitiful God. All this is supernatural, and reminds us again that the Lord's Prayer is a supernatural prayer; the prayer of the reborn, the realistic Christian who exists to do God's Will. Even so, this clause comes a long way down: after the life of worship, the life of consecration, the prayer that the soul may be fed by the hand of God. Only then is it ready for this supreme test; this quiet and genial acceptance of the wounds of life, all the deliberate injury and the casual damage that come from lack of love; this prayer from the Cross. "Love your enemies, and pray for them that persecute you." "The Saints," says St. Teresa, "rejoiced at injuries and persecutions, because in forgiving them they had something to offer God."[39]

Yet we may not put off the effort. It is to be made now. Forgive us, as we forgive; or, as another reading has it, "Forgive, and we will forgive." Not as we hope to be able to forgive presently, when our sense of God is more vivid and our sense of injury, our emotional uproar, has died down: but now. Show us, O Lord, your indulgent charity, and we will try to show it in our turn: bear with our faultiness because we are trying to love, ignoring our bruises and scratches, the small sums that are owed us, the infringements of our rights. "Having already said Thy Will be done," says St. Teresa again, "it follows that we cannot harbor any kind of grudge."[40] We can only claim the privilege of sonship because we have already admitted the unqualified rights of brotherhood; mutual tolerance and unlimited forgiveness, even in those cases, indeed especially in those cases, where violence, deceit, and injustice seem to triumph, where anger is supposed to be justified and generosity is hard. Blessed are the merciful, the generous, for they shall obtain mercy. The soul can only ask for as much as it is willing to give, or try to give. We say here that we are satisfied if God deals as gently with us at our worst as we deal with our fellows at their worst—no more. We ask to

---

39. *The Way of Perfection,* Cap. 26.

40. *The Way of Perfection,* loc. cit.

be treated as we treat them; and we must expect to
be taken at our word. Our disloyalty, selfishness,
and hardness, our failure in wide-spreading love,
with all the resultant damage, obliterated and forgotten; insofar as we have obliterated and forgotten
the disloyalty, selfishness, and hardness, the failure
in love which has marred our lives or the lives of
those we love. It becomes clear that only a very great
Christian can dare to say this prayer without qualifi-
cation. It is the acid test of a life of charity, of true
incorporation in the Body of Christ. Be perfect as
your Father in heaven is perfect; indiscriminate and
unmeasured in generosity, and in forgiving, healing
love.

> Mutual forgiveness of each vice,
> These are the gates of Paradise.

There is nothing more purifying, more redeeming than the penitent love which is awakened by the
generous forgiveness of another love. It opens a door
in the brick wall which self-esteem has built between
itself and God. But hardness and unpitying resentment are the gates of hell. There shall be weeping
and gnashing of teeth: the helpless misery of the
angry egoist.

There are two perennial situations in which the
human creature, whether individually or as a group,
has to exercise that self-oblivious charity which is
the essence of forgiveness. First the cases in which
it considers that its established rights have been

infringed—trespasses: where the vigorous self-love of others has threatened its national, social, professional, or emotional claims. Secondly the cases in which it considers that its own just demands on affection, deference, consideration, possessions, or status have not been met—debts. Either by attack or by neglect, singly or as a body, the creature's self-love, its fundamental pride, is injured; and its anger aroused. At once the walls close in; it is inevitably cut off from the society of the sons of God, and is alone with its own wrath, its own rights. But those in whom the life of prayer is operative, whose filial relation with Eternal Love is sure, are required to abandon the standpoint of self-interest whether personal or corporate; quietly and humbly to forgive the trespass, freely remit the debt, if they want to know the living peace of God. St. Teresa makes an easy and prompt forgiveness, in all the ups and downs of daily life, the very test of prayer; and thinks contemplation of little worth if we come from it able to resent anything.[41]

"Forgive us our debts." In the last resort, the soul's debt as toward God is Sanctity: for man's supernatural life, with its unspeakable possibilities, its obligations, its goal, is a trust held from the Eternal. The lord of the unmerciful bond slave forgave him a debt beyond repayment; the ten thousand talents of the parable, two million pounds and more. That too

---

41. Op. cit., loc. cit.

is the soul's situation, entrusted with the seed of sanctifying grace to cherish, the talent of holiness to increase; incorporated in the Mystical Body of the Incarnate, fed with His abundant life. It has received the unpriced gifts of the Spirit that it may bring forth the fruits of the Spirit; not in the interests of any personal beatitude, but because they are demanded by the eternal purposes of God. Love, Joy, Peace, Long-suffering: these are a part of man's debt, and here he can hardly say in his own strength, "Have patience with me and I will pay you all." Here, then, he cannot dare to say, "Pay what thou owest!" to other faulty men.

Again and again in the Gospels we find Christ insisting on the hopeless situation of the exacting, unforgiving soul, who dares to ask from God what he is not willing to give in his turn. Again and again He points out that the rigorist is a fool as well as a knave. By his own act he has put himself under the hard law of retribution which he chooses to exercise, instead of the easy and generous love which he refuses to show. For it is by the very existence of the Divine Compassion that the soul is judged. Every time that a veil is torn and it draws a little nearer to Reality, there is a fresh judgment over against the standard of God. We are judged by love, not only at the end of life, but in every crisis and opportunity of life. Everything which asks us for forgiveness judges us; and only if we pass that examination can we safely ask to be ourselves reinstated in the kingdom of love. "In making up His accounts with us," says St. Teresa, "God is never strict but always generous. However great our debt, He thinks it a small matter if through it He can gain us."[42] That generosity is the principle which runs through the New Testament. There, forgiveness is not an effort, a stern duty; but the delighted overflow of a compassionate, self-oblivious charity. It is the joy with which, after long exhausting search, the tiresome sheep is found, the lost coin hunted down; the delight of the father receiving safe and sound the worthless son who has disgraced the family name, wasted the family money, and only remembered family affection when all other resources failed. Even here, forgiveness means music and dancing; no hint of disapproval, all memory of folly and ingratitude drowned in love. Mercy and grimness cannot live together. The truly contrite soul is joyful in its shame: made glad by a confident remembrance of the infinite goodness of the Eternal, the "multitude of tender mercies" dominating its horizon and reducing to their proper proportion its poor little follies and sins.

---

42. Op. cit., loc. cit.

Chapter VIII

PREVENIENCE

Lead us not into temptation, but deliver us from evil. May that strange directive power of which from time to time we are conscious as the controlling factor of life have pity on our weakness and lead us out of confusion into peace.

This abject confession of helplessness seems at first sight to be meant for the untried and bewildered neophyte, in whom the gifts of the Spirit have not yet had time to grow. Actually, it is the culmination of the prayer which was given to the Church of God in the persons of her Apostles; those through whom the sanctification of human history was to be set going, the handful of men to whom we owe our Christian inheritance. It is this picked band, these channels of the Spirit, already surrendered to the Creative Will, who, as the very crown of filial worship, are taught to acknowledge their own fragility, their childlike status; their utter dependence on the ceaseless guiding and protecting power of God. "My times are in Thy hand. . . . Hold Thou up my going in Thy path that my footsteps slip not. . . ." All my small movements, tests, struggles, and apparent choices take place within the grasp of Creative Love. "Thou shalt answer for me, O Lord my God."

Thus the movement of prayer brings man to a

double sense of the overruling power and wisdom of God, directing at every point in small things as in great the movement of His creature, and of that creature's ignorance and weakness. If a realistic and full acknowledgment of sinfulness—the awful gap between the divine and the human—comes late in the life of prayer, later still comes this complete downfall of self-sufficiency and acceptance of our true situation. Though the soul may not seek God for any utilitarian reason, yet now at the apex of her prayer, because of her entire dependence on the unseen, she can ask with the assurance of a child for personal guidance and rescue; for the intimate concern of the Transcendent with her small and struggling life. Her faith, hope, and love converge to produce this state of abandoned trust.

The action of that overruling love fails not. It is we that resist, ignore, are lost and bewildered because we do not abandon ourselves to the steady guiding power; become lost in multiplicity, and forget the universals which condition our real life. Regret for the past, its errors and evil, and anxiety and bewilderment as regards the future, keep us enchained by succession, and our contact with the Abiding is lost. Nevertheless, as the life of prayer deepens it brings a gradual realization of the twofold character of all our experience; each event truly a part of this unceasing storm of succession, and yet each event directly linked with the quiet action of God. Through all vicissitudes of trial, sin, and conflict, the ground of the soul is rooted in His life; that country from which we are exiled, yet which is our home. For we do not in our essence belong to the world of confusion, the meaningless torrent of circumstance which so easily obsesses us. We are "sons of light and sons of the day,"[43] part of a charismatic order, members of Christ and inheritors of heaven. But we fall short of our calling, share the sin and confusion of the troubled world; which "groaneth and travaileth even until now" because of its alienation from God.

We accept that double situation with all that it involves for us. We do not ask for some impossible spirituality, some miraculous deliverance from this our creaturely state. We are committed to the life of the senses with all its risks and deceits; and we know well our own weakness, our inclination to sin. Yet we know too that in this confusion the rescuing power of the Holy is already active, and that if we are supple to His pressure we shall be kept from the temptations and delivered from the evil of a world in which grace and nature struggle together; in which the spirit of man, in spite of confusions and bewilderments, is never left alone.

The journey of the soul through life is strangely like the progress of the child Alice through Looking-glass Land. For the plot has both an active, visible, and obvious side, and a quiet, deeply hidden mysterious side. Alice, that small representative of the spirit of man, finds herself wandering through a strange, unstable world of circumstance, and undergoing many bewildering experiences which seem, as the

---

43. Rom. 8, 9.

experiences of our life often do, chaotic and unmeaning. She travels through a country which is divided like a chessboard into light and dark patches. She has no map and little sense of direction; and she passes for no apparent reason, and in no apparent sequence, from square to square. The odd people whom she meets, and the odd things which happen, seem quite unconnected with the game. Everything is in a muddle; most disconcerting to those who expect to find the clue to life's meaning in the tangle of daily events.

But if we turn back to the first page of this bewildering story, we find there what Alice wanted but could never discover: a plan of the chessboard as the Player sees it, with each piece in its right place in relation to the whole. Then we see that everything which happened to Alice, however unmeaning, disconcerting, or apparently hostile to her interests, was a real move in a real game. All these changes and chances, these pains and frustrations, were queer but deliberate devices for getting the child, who began as a pawn, to the eighth square, where she must end as a Queen. The help and direction she received from the creatures that she encountered, the imperceptible pressure of events never varied in intention. However great the obstacles, the apparent confusions and absurdities, the goal was always the eighth square. The best advice was often that which seemed most foolish; as when the Rose told Alice to walk away from the Red Queen if she wanted to meet her. The really important moves were not recognized till long after they were made. It is true that

Alice went through one of the earlier squares by train; but she was actually passing through another, almost at the end of her journey, when she thought herself hopelessly lost in the dark forest with nothing to help her but the muddled statements of the White Knight. Once she was called right off the path to befriend the silly and untidy old White Queen. Yet it was in running after the Queen's lost shawl, and jumping the little brook over which it had floated, that Alice made her next move, and reached the fifth square. Here we easily recognize our own experience; and so too in that puzzling phase when life sometimes seemed to Alice to be a shop full of possessions, and sometimes to be a river on which she had to row. When it seemed to be a shop, the egg moved away directly she wanted to buy it; and when she looked hard at anything, it ceased to be real. When it seemed to be a river, the flowering rush that she wanted was always just out of reach, and those she managed to pick soon faded and died. Yet in spite of her bewilderment the child caught in the web of circumstance was never really lost; each baffling experience contributed something to the whole. The hand of the Player was hovering over the pawn.

This seems a childish allegory to use as the veil of so great a mystery; the ultimate mystery of faith. But its inner meaning gives new significance to the jumble of incidents, the alternation of drift and bustle, the competing claims, the griefs and joys, the errors and recoveries, frustrations and compulsions, which seem to make up most of our life. "That thou being our ruler and guide we may so pass through things temporal"—the dark and light patches, field and forest, and sudden changes that lead to a new square—"that we lose not the things that be eternal": our constant hold on Thine unchanging presence, our dependence on Thy wisdom and love. "Deliver us from evil"—not from the pain and trial which test and brace us, but from all that can damage our relation to Thee. "It is faith," says Grou, "which says this prayer; and faith recognizes only those supernatural evils which wound the Holiness of God and tarnish the purity of the soul."[44]

The way on which we are set is difficult and obscure; the friction of life, the action of others, and our own tangled and inordinate desires make ceaseless demands on our patience and courage. We are often fed on bitter and unappetizing food: are invited to envy and covetousness, ambition and pride—all the unpurified energies of our lower nature struggling for expression. But the calm splendor of God penetrates, overrules, harmonizes all this changing experience. We ask to be kept in remembrance of that; especially in those crucial moments when the mystery seems too great, bewilderment overwhelms us, and we are tempted to lose our nerve. Natural man partakes of the struggles and confusions of the natural order. Everything about

---

44. J. N. Grou, *L'Ecole de Jésus Christ,* 39ième Leçon.

him contradicts the Eternal. But the man of prayer, because of his personal adherence to God, asks to be delivered from all that:

In thee, O Lord, have I put my trust, let me never be
  put to confusion:
But rid me and deliver me in thy righteousness; incline
  thine ear unto me and save me.[45]

It is from our own evil tendencies above all, our inveterate egotism with its million cunning disguises, our pride, greed, and anger, our steady downward drag to self-satisfaction that we need deliverance: for this we can never vanquish in our own strength. Do not let us be swamped in the strange tumult and conflict: the evil that results from the clash of wills unharmonized with Thy will. Deliver us by keeping clear that single relation with Thee which is our peace. We want the firm resistance of the overruling Spirit always present in the soul's deeps to the sudden up-rushes from lower centers of consciousness, the personal devils lodging in the basement, the interior hurly-burly of desires and dislikes; so easily aroused, so hard to quell. Our amphibious state is so delicately poised, so perilous, that only help from the higher can save us from being conquered by the lower. Deliver us from our share in the world's sin, our twist away from Holiness; reinforcing by your energetic grace our feeble will toward the good. We

---

45. Ps. 31, 1, 2.

have reached now a vivid consciousness of "that deep abyss of perversity" of which de Caussade speaks, into which, with so many others, we should fall if God did not hold us. "It is only through their practical knowledge of this, taught by a repeated personal experience, that the Saints have acquired that fundamental humility, that utter contempt and holy hatred of themselves of which we see so many proofs in their lives, and which have been the true source of their perfection."[46] With them we ask that our divergent lives may be brought into line with that one Life in which evil did not operate; which escaped the doom laid upon this planet, and even in the extremity of suffering never faltered in its perfect response to the Father's Will.

Thus the movement of prayer brings the soul to this realization and this petition; to the status of a supernatural creature, tightly bound in this present life to all the vicissitudes of succession, yet deeply aware of its own distinctness and its own true life as consisting in a total dependence, the closest of personal links with Creative Love. That being so, it must commit itself without reserve to the hidden directive power; not presuming to ask that it may be tested to the uttermost, knowing its own fragility and the perils which wait for presumptuous souls. This is the life of faith; and in the consummation of faith, the life of prayer is fulfilled. "In faith," says

---

46. De Caussade, *L'Abandon à la Providence Divine,* Vol. I, p. 229.

Kierkegaard, "the self bases itself transparently on the power which created it."[47] The whole life of prayer is indeed a committal of our separate lives into God's hand, a perpetual replacing of the objective attitude by the personal and abandoned attitude: and though a certain tension, suffering, and bewilderment are inevitable to our situation, yet there is with this a deep security. The pawn does not know what will be required of it or what may be before it; but its relation with the Player is always direct and stable, and the object of the Player is always the good of the pawn. "Our souls are God's delight, not because of anything they do for Him, but because of what He does for them. All He asks of them is to accept with joy His indulgence, His generosity, His fatherly love. Consider all your devotion to God in this way, and do not worry any more about what you are or are not. Be content to be the object of His mercy and look at nothing else."[48]

"Lead us not into temptation." Temptation is that sphere in which the evil dispositions which are present in the world—its whole trend toward self-satisfaction, self-fulfillment, and away from God—appear in their attractiveness and dominate the situation. We are not to presume on our strength and deliberately seek contact with that. This spoils the

---

47. Kierkegaard: *Die Krankheit zum Tode* ["The Sickness Unto Death"], p. 11.

48. De Tourville. *Pensées Diverses,* p. 95.

perfection of our meek abandonment to the Spirit; the subordination of our restless will to the steady pressure of God. To live by faith is to pursue quietly and in peace the path on which we are set, in the midst of the conflicts and confusions of the creature. In that quiet subordination is fullness of life; not in the passion for self-expression which tries every situation and every relationship and confuses pride with courage and initiative.

Christ seems to have been deeply aware of the fragility of human nature; the folly of heroics, the danger of demanding or attempting too much. Watch and pray, that ye enter not into temptation. The spirit may be willing; but do not forget your lowly origin, the flesh is weak. Therefore, even in your abandonment, remain spiritually alert. Watch steadily. Gaze at God: keep your minds attuned to His reality and His call, and so elude the distractions that surround you. Pray. Seek His face. Lift up to Him your heart and speak to Him as one friend to another. Reach out toward Him in confident love. "By two wings," says Thomas à Kempis, "is man borne up from earthly things, that is to say with plainness and cleanness: plainness is in the intent and cleanness is in the love. The good, true, and plain intent looketh toward God, but the clean love maketh assay and tasteth his sweetness."[49] So doing, you are drawn more and more deeply into His life,

---

49. *The Imitation of Christ.* Bk. III, Chap. 4.

and have less and less to fear from competing attractions, longings, and demands.

The crucial moment for the soul is not when the crown of jewels and the crown of thorns are set before it, as before St. Catherine of Siena, and it is required to choose between them. Here none but the utterly unloving could hesitate. It is the moment when it comes suddenly on the crown of jewels in its full attraction, and does not see the crown of thorns. To watch and pray means such a quiet and steady concentration on the Eternal as defends us against these perilous moments; and with this an acceptance of weakness and limitation, a meek willingness to learn that way of prudence which is taught by the Wisdom of God. It means putting aside all ambition to find out how much we can endure; being docile and avoiding the path which is for us marked "dangerous," even though it be a path that has been trodden by the saints. Our idea of our own power of resistance usually exceeds what we shall really manage when the pinch comes. "If all shall be offended in thee, I shall never be offended!" said St. Peter. We know what happened to the one who said that. All we dare to ask is that God will reinforce our will by the energy of His grace, and bring us safely through those normal temptations which none escape.

Nor does this humble moderation, this matter-of-fact dependence, which is the final position of the developing life of prayer, come to us from a religion of Safety First. It is the teaching of One who knew in the wilderness the full temptation which comes with the possession of great powers, and in Gethsemane the awful face-to-face encounter with the forces of destruction, the horror and trembling of spirit before approaching agony, darkness, and death. So austere, so arduous is the Christian program, so real the struggle and so rough the journey to which the soul is called, that only when guided by a Spirit who knows the route better than we do, can we hope to get through without disaster. Any self-willed addition to life's difficulties brings its own punishment. There will be plenty of opportunity for courage, staying power, and initiative as well as for humble obedience, for those who follow the guide's footsteps and are docile to His direction; some narrow ledges and treacherous slopes before we finish. All will be well if we do not yield to the temptation to tackle them alone; but there is every reason to fear the attractive shortcut, the opportunity to satisfy our thirst for private spiritual adventure. The saints were driven on by rough tracks and awful darkness, in suffering and loneliness, by cloud and storm. They reached the summits; but never in their own strength or by following their own ideas—often indeed by taking what seems to onlookers the most unlikely route, because their feet were set upon a supernatural path which others cannot see.

What a deep and beautiful confidence it means if we are to accept this truth; not as a religious notion, but as the most massive fact of our strange mixed life, the culmination of our prayer. The ultimate humble trust of the little creature which first dared to say Abba, Father, is placed in the Absolute Love; and finds in the simple return to God the Unchanging, that personal and permanent relation which is the ground of prayer, the sovereign remedy against temptation, and defense against the assaults of the world's ill.

Thine is the Kingdom, the Power, and the Glory. The prayer in which is contained the whole movement of man's interior life, the substance of his communion with God, is summed up in this delighted declaration of the independent perfection, the unspeakable transcendence of the Holy. Before that reality, that majesty, that energy, that splendor, his own needs, his own significance, vanish. Abba, Father. It is true that the Infinite God is the Father of my soul, that I have a certain kinship with the Abiding, a privilege of cooperation. Higher than my highest, He is yet nearer than my inmost part. But in the last resort, I stand entranced and abased before the majesty, the otherness of that Infinite God.

"He calleth the stars by their names." All things, all mysteries, are brought to Him as their test and meaning. Thine is the Kingdom, hidden from our sight yet already present in perfection; Thy secret rule working from within, Thine unseen pattern imposed on our chaos, Thy Spirit brooding on the deep, turning all things to Thy purpose, and even through conflicts, sin, and anguish conditioning and transforming every aspect of human life. Thine is the Power, the inexhaustible energy streaming forth from Thy hidden Being, by which the universe visible and invisible is sustained. Thine is the Glory, the self-revealed splendor of the Eternal Perfect filling and transcending creation; seen in its humblest beauties, yet never fully known. We look beyond the ramparts of the world to that triune Reality, the goal of our faith, hope, and love.

On all this, at the end of its prayer, the eyes of the faithful soul are opened. Here life is lost and found again in God. The whole drive of will and desire is carried out beyond the changing of the Changeless; and summed up in Him, our only need. More and more, acts and petitions fall from us. The agony of our supplication is silenced, and one simple and confident movement of surrender to the total purpose takes its place. We end on the acknowledgment that all we can see, love, and delight in, all that crushes and bewilders, shames, or reassures us, is nothing beside that which we do not and cannot comprehend: "the mystery which from all ages hath been hid in God."[50]

Glory, said the Rabbis—that brightness on the face of man, in which the created order gave back a faint reflection of the Eternal Radiance—was the first thing lost by Adam at the Fall. But through the incarnation of the Holy in that created order, it is restored to humanity in Christ. "We beheld His glory, the glory of the Only Begotten full of grace and truth." He is the "first and only fair," the sacramental disclosure of the Beauty of God. By one of

---

50. Eph. 3, 9.

the strange reversals which are the peculiar secret of love, the supreme manifestation upon earth of that Absolute Beauty is seen in the sacrifice of the Cross; the Perfect, the Strong, the Radiant, self-offered for the sinful, the murky, the weak, and achieving His victory through suffering, failure, death. On the face of the Crucified "the light of the knowledge of the glory of God" is revealed.[51] Here then we reach the summit of man's prayer, in this recognition of the self-existent supernatural Glory, the radiance of Reality lying beyond us, yet already with us and awaiting us. In this we achieve an entire release from the earth-centered life with its disharmonies and griefs, its fears and cravings, and anchor our souls in the Unchanging. "Through faith," says St. Paul, "we stand already in grace. But we look towards glory";[52] and in that contemplation we are already gathered into the liberty of the children of God.

Glory is the final word of religion, as joy is its final state. The sparks and trickles of the Supernatural which come to us, the hints received through beauty and through sacrifice, the mysterious visitations and pressures of grace reaching us through conflicts, rebellions, and torments of the natural world—all these are earnests of a Perfection, a Wholeness yet unseen: as the small range of sound and color revealed by the senses witness to the unseen color and unheard music of a Reality which lies beyond

---

51. 2 Cor. 4, 6.

52. Rom. 5, 2.

their narrow span. All within the created order points beyond itself, to the uncreated Kingdom, Power, and Glory. No life, no intelligence reaches perfection; yet in each there is a promise of the Perfect. Each comes up to its limit, and in so doing testifies to that which lies beyond it; the unlimited splendor of the Abiding, the Glory of the living God. So too the creature's prayer comes up to its limit, and ends upon a word, a reality, which we can neither define nor apprehend.

All thy works praise thee, O Lord,
And thy saints give thanks unto thee.
They shew the glory of thy kingdom,
And talk of thy power:
That thy power, thy glory, and mightiness of thy
   kingdom
Might be known to men.[53]

Yet even this Kingdom, Power, and Glory, this threefold manifestation of the character of God, is not ultimate. The appeal of man's prayer is to a Reality which is beyond manifestation. All these are Thine; but we reach out to Thee. Beyond the wall of contradiction, beyond the "Light that is not God," almost imperceptible to the attentive creature and yet the ground of its being and goal of its prayer, is the secret Presence; the Thou in whom all things inhere, by whom all live. Behind every closed door

---

53. Ps. 145, 10–12.

which seems to shut experience from us He is standing; and within every experience which reaches us, however disconcerting, His unchanging presence is concealed. Not in the wind which sweeps over the face of existence to change it, not in the earthquake which makes sudden havoc of our ordered life, not in the overwhelming splendor and fury of the elemental fire: in none of these, but in the "voice of gentle stillness," speaking from within the agony and bewilderment of life, we recognize the presence of the Holy and the completing answer to the soul's completed prayer. We accept Thy Majesty, we rejoice in Thy Power and Thy Glory; but in Thine unchanging quiet is our trust. We looked beyond the spiritual to Spirit, beyond the soul's country to the personal Origin and Father of its life.

"This is our Lord's will," says Julian of Norwich, "that our prayer and our trust be both alike large."[54] Step by step we have ascended the hill of the Lord; and here at the summit of our beseeching, conscious of our own littleness and the surrounding mystery, we reach out in confidence to the All. The last phase of prayer carries the soul forward to an entire self-oblivion, an upward and outward glance of awestruck worship which is yet entinctured with an utter and childlike trust. Abba, Father. Thine is the Kingdom, the Power, and the Glory. Thou art the Beginning and the End of the soul's life.

---

54. *Revelations of Divine Love,* Cap. 42.

SUGGESTIONS FOR FURTHER READING

SELECTED WORKS BY EVELYN UNDERHILL

The Church and War. London: Anglican Pacifist Fellowship, 1940.

Evelyn Underhill Estate. *Collected Papers.* Longmans, Green & Co., 1946.

Concerning the Inner Life. London: Methuen & Co., 1926.

The Fruits of the Spirit. London: Longmans, Green & Co., 1942.

The House of the Soul. London: Methuen & Co., 1929.

The Life of the Spirit and the Life of Today. London: Methuen & Co., 1922. Published by Morehouse Publishing, Harrisburg, PA, in the series Library of Anglican Spirituality, 1994.

Evelyn Underhill Estate. *Light of Christ.* London: Longmans, Green & Co., 1944.

Man and the Supernatural. London: Methuen & Co., 1927.

A Meditation on Peace. London: Fellowship of Reconciliation, 1939.

Mixed Pastures. London: Methuen & Co., 1933.

Evelyn Underhill Estate. *The Mount of Purification.* London: Longmans, Green & Co., 1949.

Mysticism. London: Methuen, 1911.

Mysticism. Twelfth edn. New York: New American Library, 1974.

The Mystics of the Church. Cambridge: J. Clarke, 1925. Republished by Morehouse Publishing, Harrisburg, PA, in the series Library of Anglican Spirituality, 1975.

The School of Charity. London: Longmans, Green & Co., 1934.

The Spiritual Life. London: Hodder & Stoughton, 1937 (current edition: Mowbray, 1984).

Worship. London: Nisbet, 1936 (current edition: Eagle, 1991).

THE EVELYN UNDERHILL ASSOCIATION (EUA)

See the web site for the Evelyn Underhill Association at http://www.evelynunderhill.org/life.htm. (Most of the books listed above, as well as other titles, are available from the EUA bookstore.)

BOOKS ABOUT EVELYN UNDERHILL

Armstrong, Christopher. *Evelyn Underhill.* London and Oxford: Mowbray, 1975.

Brame, Grace (ed.). *The Ways of the Spirit: Four Retreats Given by Evelyn Underhill.* New York: Crossroad, 1990.

Callahan, Annice. *Evelyn Underhill: Spirituality for

Daily Living. Lanham, MD: University Press of America, 1997.

Cropper, Margaret. *Life of Evelyn Underhill.* New York: Harper, 1958.

Egan, Harvey, S. J. *An Anthology of Christian Mysticism.* Collegeville, MN: The Liturgical Press, 1996.

————. *What Are They Saying About Mysticism?* Mahwah, NJ: Paulist Press, 1982.

Greene, Dana. *Evelyn Underhill: Artist of the Infinite Life.* New York: Crossroad, 1990.

————. *Modern Guide to the Ancient Quest for the Holy.* Albany: State University of New York Press, 1988.

Hartill, Percy (ed.). *Into the Way of Peace.* London: James Clark, 1940.

Jantzen, Grace. "The Legacy of Evelyn Underhill." *Feminist Theology* 4 (Sept. 1993): 79–100.

Kelsey, Morton. *The Other Side of Silence.* London: SPCK, 1976.

Underhill, Arthur. *Change and Decay.* London: Butterworth & Co., 1938.

Williams, Charles (ed.). *The Letters of Evelyn Underhill.* London: Longmans, Green & Co., 1943.

CAROL ZALESKI is Professor of Religion at Smith College. She is the author of *Otherworld Journeys* (1987) and *The Life of the World to Come* (1996). With her husband, Philip Zaleski, she is the editor of *The Book of Heaven: An Anthology of Writings from Ancient to Modern Times* (2000).

JOHN F. THORNTON is a literary agent, former book editor, and the coeditor, with Katharine Washburn, of *Dumbing Down* (1996) and *Tongues of Angels, Tongues of Men: A Book of Sermons* (1999). He lives in New York City.

SUSAN B. VARENNE is a New York City high school teacher with a strong avocational interest in and wide experience of spiritual literature (M.A., University of Chicago Divinity School; Ph.D., Columbia University).